# THE
# RADIO
# CONTROL
# MODEL MANUAL

As part of our ongoing market research, we are always pleased to receive comments about our books, suggestions for new titles, or requests for catalogues. Please write to:
The Editorial Director, Patrick Stephens Limited, Sparkford, Near Yeovil, Somerset BA22 7JJ.

# THE RADIO CONTROL MODEL MANUAL

## A step-by-step guide to the remote operation of models

## DAVID BODDINGTON

Patrick Stephens Limited

First published in 1995

British Library Cataloguing-in-Publication Data:
A catalogue record for this book is available from the British Library

ISBN 1 85260 480 8

Library of Congress catalog card number 95–79122

Patrick Stephens Limited is an imprint of
Haynes Publishing,
Sparkford, Nr Yeovil, Somerset.
BA22 7JJ, England

Typeset by J.H. Haynes & Co Ltd
Printed in Great Britain by J.H. Haynes & Co Ltd

**While every effort is taken to ensure the accuracy of the information given in
this book, no liability can be accepted by the author or publishers for any loss,
damage or injury caused by errors in, or omissions from, the information given.**

# Contents

# Preface

As a boy I made many types of models, from the card Micromodels of galleons and locomotives to the OO gauge, 4 mm to the foot scale vehicles (yes, there were metric/imperial measurement problems 50 years ago) to accompany railway layouts. Model boats were only of real interest if they floated and moved under their own power, whether this was achieved by a piece of camphor, a wound up rubber band, a clockwork motor purloined from another toy or, most wonderfully, by a working steam engine. However, my main preoccupation was with model aeroplanes, initially with solid wooden models, before plastics came on to the scene, then with flying models of various types. The fascination of designing, making and operating miniature replica machinery has never left me.

All of these early models boats, vehicles and aeroplanes were 'free running'; in other words, once they had been released you had no control over them. Certainly you could set the wheels of a car so that it would continue to run in circles, a model yacht could have

*In the pre-radio-control days models were either static or 'free running'. Some of the author's models are displayed on exhibition in the mid-1940s.*

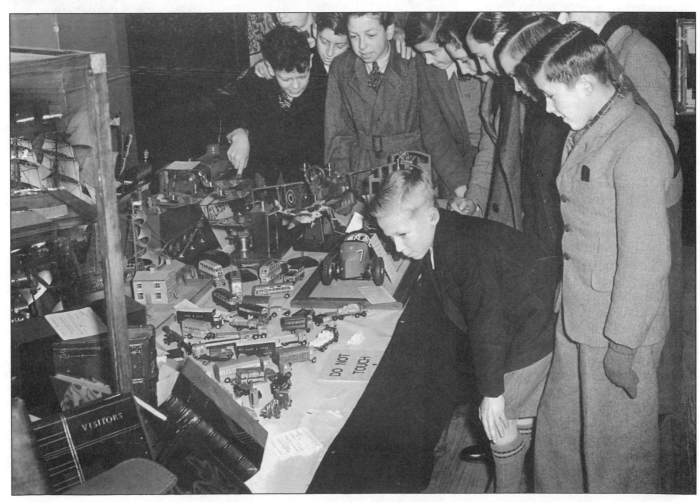

the sails and rudder set so that it would cross a lake in a virtually straight line, and a model aeroplane could be set up so that – hopefully – it would climb in circles under power and – equally hopefully – would circle in the opposite direction to earth. All too often the model aeroplane would crash to earth before you reached the point of correctly trimming the model to complete a full flight with a reasonable landing.

The frustrations of being restricted to circular patterns, or the very real risk of crashes at the end of a straight run, were very considerable. Model cars, powered by small spark ignition or diesel engines, could be tethered to a steel cable and allowed to revolve around a central post; this was fine for pure speed events, but no good for general sports operation. The same style of running was used for model hydroplanes and speed boats.However, my constant schoolboy dream was to be able to take the model out and make it move in the direction I wanted it to go. A model tank that would climb the sand traps and move over the lawn to the garden bed, and might even have a working gun that could be turned on the neighbour's dog (I had a strong suspicion that it had chewed up one of my gliders); boats and ships that could be brought into harbour; and it might even be possible to make a submarine that would submerge – and return to the surface! Dreams they had to remain, at least for the moment, but boyhood dreams can become manhood reality.

Partial control of model aircraft came with the introduction of control line ('U control') models where the aeroplane was connected by two lines, usually thin wire, to a control handle. Moving the control handle up or

*Two early non-radio-controlled models built by the author, a control-line K. K. 'Skystreak' and a free-flight Fokker D8 model powered by a 0.5 cc diesel engine.*

down caused, through a system of bellcranks and horns, the elevator on the tailplane (stabiliser) to hinge up and down, thus making the model climb or dive. Indeed, it was possible to get the aeroplane to loop, perform horizontal figures of eight and fly inverted, if the correct design of model was used and the pilot was skilled. There remained, though, the proviso that the model rotated continuously around the operator to keep the control lines taut and to allow the elevator to be moved accurately. Once the lines went slack all degree of control was lost and the model would crash.

In my quest for control of model aeroplanes I devised a system utilising an air operated cylinder, which would slowly move through its piston operating length, connected to a cam. The cam followers were linked to the elevator and rudder, the theory being that the arrangement would set the model's control surfaces to positions where it would climb to a safe height, then initiate a number of manoeuvres, including moderate turns, a dive and terminating, before landing, in a loop. It took a long time to develop the system and to attain precisely

the correct degree of movement of the control surfaces. With one cam design I achieved reasonable success until on one flight the engine did not produce enough power, the climb took the model to only a marginal height, and when the cam introduced the dive, the ground was too close! Back to the drawing board.

It was during the five years spent training as an architect and two and a half years training as a pilot in the RAF that the answer to my dreams became reality – commercially available radio control equipment.

*During my period training in the RAF, radio control equipment became more commercially available – I soloed on a jet before I did with a radio-controlled model!*

# Introduction

It would be wrong to give the impression that the use of radio control, even with models, is a new thing, it is not. A music hall (vaudeville) act before the First World War used a very primitive form of radio control to allow them to 'sail' a helium-filled model airship out into the auditorium, then steer it back to the stage. Radio control aircraft, not much smaller than manned fighters, were flown, or attempts were made to fly them, in the First World War, and in the 1930s manned aircraft were converted to radio control operation. One of the best known aeroplanes of this type was the 'Queen Bee', which was essentially a De Havilland DH82A 'Tiger Moth' fitted with radio control to operate the rudder, elevator, ailerons and engine throttle. The controller sat on the ground at his console and the aircraft was flown within visual distances and used for target practice by army and naval guns.

The equipment used for military purposes was reasonably reliable, but was far too heavy, not to say expensive, for our modelling purposes. Further improvements and experiments were made during the Second World War, the German Air Force developing a radio controlled bomb that was guided to its target by the operator sitting in the glazed nose of the bomber carrier. The guided bomb was in the form of a glider with a warhead, and was not powered in any way.

*Single-channel equipment only operated one function, normally rudder control. The airborne equipment consisted of a battery pack, receiver and switch and actuator, either rubber-driven or clockwork.*

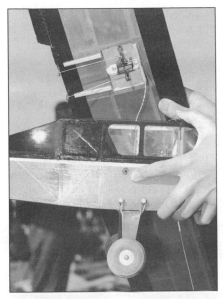

*Rubber-driven escapements eventually gave way to motorised servos. Note that the wing of the 'Flapper' first had an Elmic Conquest escapement, with the rubber motor extending down the wing panel, then the Hinode servo, with a five-wire connection.*

It was the American Good brothers who pioneered radio control systems in model aeroplanes in the late 1930s, but it was not until the end of the Second World War that any practical form of radio control equipment became available to the average modeller. Even then the word 'average' had to be taken to mean a modeller so keen on the subject that he was prepared to sacrifice many of his other interests – and responsibilities – to follow this aspect of his hobby.

In common with other forms of electronic equipment, such as television, radio, audio reproduction and video, progress has been made steadily over the years, it did not just appear overnight. Nor was the use of radio control restricted to model aeroplanes, its functions and purposes were equally recognised by boat enthusiasts, it allowed the development of on and off road car racing, provided remote controlling of railway points, signals and locomotives, and eventually led, in 1970, to a successfully controlled model helicopter. The latter challenge proved to be one of the most difficult problems to be solved. Radio control has also proved a boon to model submarine enthusiasts for the control of their sub-aqua designs, although I remain to be convinced that diving into a murky pool, losing visual contact, then guessing where the model will re-emerge, is quite the degree of control we should be looking for.

Of course the common factor in all of these branches of our radio control hobby is the precise control of the model to suit our desires – that dream again. With modern radio control equipment it is possible to emulate the manoeuvres of pretty well any full-

11

*'Reed' equipment was non-proportional, but did allow more than one control to be operated simultaneously. However, you invariably found yourself short of fingers to operate the multitude of switches.*

size vehicle, boat or plane. Indeed, we can often perform manoeuvres that their larger brothers are unable to carry out – witness an R/C (radio control) model helicopter flying inverted a few inches above the ground, or performing 'head-over-heels' manoeuvres within touching distance of the operator. It was not always so.

In the early days of commercial radio control for models, there were two basic types of equipment, known as 'single channel' and 'reeds'. Single channel was only capable of giving one control

function, for example the rudder of a boat or aeroplane, and this control was not proportional. All that could be achieved was a full movement of the rudder in one direction followed, on the release of the signal, by a return to the neutral position; the next signal would move the rudder in the opposite direction. With some of the equipment being of 'super-regen' and not 'superhet' design, it was only possible to fly one model at a time. In spite of these obvious limitations, a great deal of satisfaction and enjoyment could be obtained from the use of this

basic equipment; indeed it would still be a mistake to think that complexity and cost equate with pleasure and enjoyment.

'Reed' radio control was so called because of the reed bank fitted in the radio receiver, with each reed being tuned, harmonically, to a specific transmitted signal. By using the harmonics on the transmitted signal, it was possible to control specific functions by amplifying the signal from the individual reed switch on the bank and driving a servo mechanism. Thus a 12-switch reed bank would give you

*Magnetic actuators and miniature transistorised single-function receivers allowed for simple control of very small, light models, but wiring of actuators, switches and batteries was still the prerogative of the modeller.*

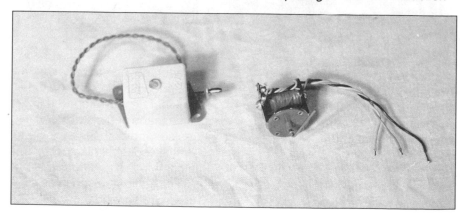

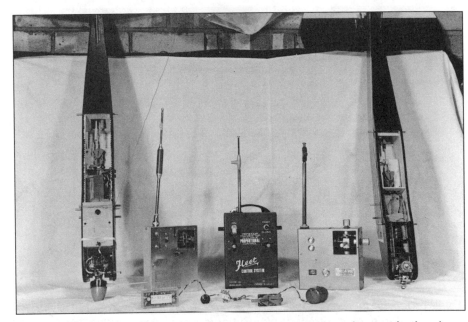

*Pulse proportional equipment (known as 'Galloping Ghost') was the poor man's proportional equipment in the days when the full proportional outfit cost a month's wages. The Rand actuator was a very clever device and provided rudder and elevator control, with the control surfaces continually oscillating but dwelling longer in one position, and rudimentary engine throttle control.*

six functions, operated by six two-way switches on the transmitter. Rudder, elevator, aileron and engine throttle control were available, plus, say, elevator trim (small adjustments around the neutral) and the operation of the retracting undercarriage. However, the controls were still only on/off and not proportional, but this was possibly of less hindrance to boat operators, where the models were slower, than it was to aviators and racing car enthusiasts.

Operating the six twin direction transmitter switches has been likened to playing the Bach Toccata and Fugue on a piped organ. The fingers had to be exceptionally nimble to get the right amount of movement, the switch had to be pulsed rapidly to give an intermediate control position, and with at least three of the switches needing constant operation you were always short of thumbs. When my brother and I first attempted to fly a model fitted with 12-channel (six-function) reed

equipment, we looked at the transmitter and decided that it must be impossible for one person to operate all the controls, so my brother took the left hand switches and I took the right hand bank. The only problem was that the rudder switch was on the left and the aileron on the right – we finished up going sideways into a house!

The advent of proportional equipment, where the servos and control surfaces move in direct proportion to the movement of the transmitter sticks or levers, caused a great deal of excitement. Very high costs caused the development of a cheaper, but very restricted, form of proportional equipment, known as 'pulse proportional', but this only lasted until full proportional radio equipment became available at affordable prices.

Pulse proportional R/C equipment, using a magnetic actuator, did survive longer than most, however, as it offered two advantages: low cost and low

installation weight. This allowed small models, placed in the car boot out of the way of the wife's eyes, to be taken out when larger models would have been forbidden! It is possible that, for the very lightest weight of R/C airborne equipment – weight being of greater consequence in aeroplanes than in other types of models – a pulse proportional system may still offer a slight advantage. Miniaturisation of fully proportional receivers, servos and batteries is now developing rapidly, so even that possible advantage will soon be eroded.

Incidentally, you may wonder why it should be necessary to concern ourselves with such degrees of miniaturisation. Indoor R/C flying, table top car racing (not going round on a manufactured track) and even submarines in the bath become possibilities.

The advent of modern proportional equipment means that gone are the days, thank goodness, when the modeller was

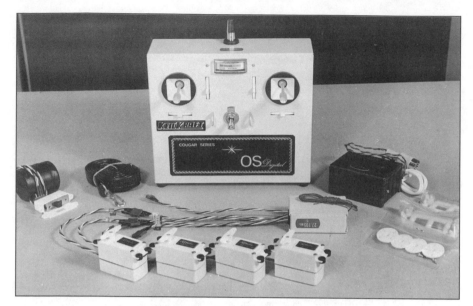

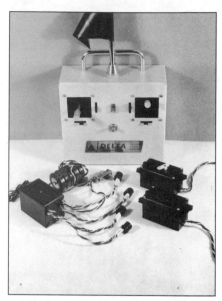

*Early proportional radio equipment was, by today's standards, bulky and basic, just the four principal functions being available, plus trim controls. But at least we were getting into the era of pre-wired equipment, the servos, receiver, switch and battery being fitted with plugs and sockets.*

expected to make the wiring harnesses between the battery, switch, servos and receiver. You had to be quite a whiz-kid with the soldering iron to finish up with a neat installation and a reasonable degree of reliability. Today you go

into your local model shop, decide which outfit you require, or can afford, and come away with it ready to install directly into your model and plug in to charge the batteries. At this point I should give a warning. Modern radio control

outfits are very attractive in their own right, they are beautifully packaged and presented, and the model shop salesman will probably switch the equipment on to show you how well it operates. It is indeed very desirable – it even

*A few of the radio-controlled models that were 'an impossible dream' in the pre-radio days. From fire-breathing dragons to flying horses, from giant 'Concordes', 'Stealth' fighters and the mightiest of B-52 'Big Buff' jet bombers and transports to tiny twin-engined 'Mosquitos', boats, ships and vehicles of all descriptions, even trains and trams – all are now possible with modern radio equipment*

smells attractive – but it should always be remembered that it is only there for a purpose, to allow us to control remotely our models; it does not have a life of its own. Never be seduced into buying equipment because you want it, only buy if you need it. The same is true when considering obsolescence of equipment; R/C equipment is only obsolete if it no longer does the job required, is no longer reliable, or cannot be repaired or serviced. It is not obsolete just because some new equipment has come on to the market.

In the Preface I wrote of myself,

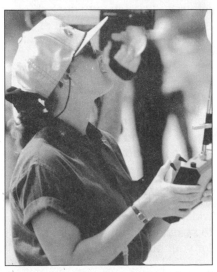

*A hobby for all, young and old, male and female – and magicians, like Paul Daniels.*

*The rough layout for the cover of an early edition of* Radio Control Models & Electronics, *one of the first specialist magazines to be published and still a leader in the market.*

as a very young modeller, having dreams of being able to control my models by remote control. All of these dreams are now a practical proposition, and it might be thought that the realisation of these dreams has diminished the enjoyment and reduced the horizons of the hobby. Far from it. The radio equipment is merely a means to an end, allowing us to fulfil our dreams and to achieve the building and operation of models that we would have previously considered impossible. Unless you happened to have been a radio and electronics enthusiast and enjoyed the building of the radio control equipment, we can only thank and praise the designers and technicians for producing such great equipment. It certainly surpasses my wildest dreams, and I have no doubt that there are many more surprises to come.

One fact I should make clear is that although this is a manual, it does not deal with the repair and servicing of radio control equipment. The electronics and, to a lesser degree, the mechanics of the transmitter, receiver and servos are highly specialised, and in the days of micro-processors, integrated circuits and sealed motors there is a minimum of self servicing that can be undertaken by the amateur owner. What *is* important is to understand how the equipment works, its limitations, advantages and disadvantages, how to install the model-borne equipment and how to obtain the best results from radio control. In addition, knowing the various types of models that can be controlled by radio control will widen your horizons and help you to select the right radio equipment for your purposes.

# Chapter 1

# The Outfit

Radio control is a method of controlling, remotely, a model either simply, by using only one control function, such as for steering, or with more complexity, where many functions are utilised to achieve the movements and effects desired in simulating a prototype. Irrespective of the complexity of the radio control system, the equipment can be sub-divided into two parts:

1  Ground equipment –
   the transmitter

2  The airborne system –
   the receiver and decoder plus the electro-mechanical devices (servos) for actuating the controls.

In addition to these basics are required switches, batteries and wiring extension leads, plus a charger for the batteries of the receiver and transmitter.

## Radio control explained – transmitter, receiver and servo

To understand how controls from the operator, via the transmitter, can be sent and accepted by the receiver, and passed on to the servos to actuate movement to the required degree, we can take a look at the simplified explanation of the workings of a digital proportional system.

In a 'digital' radio system things can be made a little simpler to comprehend by likening the process to a movie film. In the latter a series of still pictures or 'frames' are projected in rapid succession, each one depicting the position or size of moving objects at one particular moment during this movement. The resulting effect on the screen is a continuous moving picture, the staccato effect of the pictures being 'smoothed' out by the human eye. Similarly, in a 'digital' system the transmitter is a 'projector' sending out information in a continuous stream of 'frames' of equal duration, but this time it is radio energy and not light that is

being transmitted. A complete 'frame' consists of a series of periods or pulses of energy, formed by switching the radio signal on and off rapidly at determined intervals.

The duration of each period of transmission and the next and the breaks between them are controlled by one of the sticks on the transmitter; thus if there are four breaks there will be three independently variable periods of transmission or 'pulses' between them. If a stick is moved, the corresponding pulse will increase or decrease proportionally in each successive 'frame' transmitted. To complete the 'frames', after all the pulses have been transmitted a

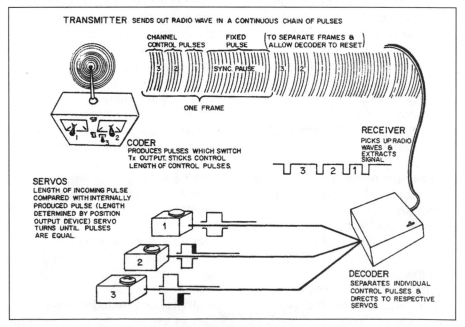

*A diagrammatic sketch showing the operating sequence of a digital proportional outfit, as described in a MacGregor instruction booklet.*

pause or fixed period of uninterrupted signal is added in order to separate successive 'frames' and enable the decoding electronics in the receiver to reset in order to be able to accept the next 'frame'. In practice, tens of 'frames' are produced in each second.

Let us move on now to the receiving end. It would be a little difficult in such a simple discussion to explain how the complex 'superhet' receiver picks up the radio signal and processes it. Therefore it will suffice to say that the receiver simply acts like a switch – it is 'on' when it receives a pulse and goes 'off' in between each pulse. Thus the result is a chain of 'ons' and 'offs', still in 'frames' and still exactly following the orders as given out by the transmitter. This information is then passed to the decoder, which, by a process used in computers termed 'logic', separates the individual control pulses in each 'frame'. In the case we considered, using three-channel equipment, we would have three quite separate chains of pulses from three independent outputs, each chain consisting of one of the three pulses in the original separated by a fixed 'off' period.

The final link in the system is the servo. Here the pulses from the transmitter, which it should be remembered are still variable, are compared with a similar pulse produced internally by the servo. The internal pulse and its duration is controlled by the position of the output arm. If the input pulses are longer or shorter than the internal comparison pulse, the servo is driven in one direction or the other, until the servo corrects the discrepancy and hence comes to rest. As with the film, the 'frames' are produced so fast that resultant action is continuous and extremely sensitive.

## Frequencies

The 'projected' information being sent out from the transmitter is in the form of high-frequency carrier waves, and this frequency is controlled and determined by using a 'crystal'.

Very precise frequency control is necessary for modellers' radio equipment, as the government radio regulatory bodies of various countries only allocate relatively narrow wavebands for our purposes. To allow us to operate more than one model at a time we therefore subdivide the available frequency band width into 'spot' frequencies of close spacing. It is essential that the transmitters and receivers are closely controlled to these 'spot' frequencies by the use of crystals, cut to oscillate at very precise resonances, although future radio control equipment may rely more on the use of synthesised frequency control, where the frequency required can simply be 'dialled' into the equipment. This technology is already with us and it is only the practical application that is preventing its widespread use.

A system has to be devised whereby the frequency of our R/C equipment cannot be changed without due regard to any other modeller already transmitting on that frequency. Making it more easy to change transmitter frequencies may seem to be a great advantage, but the physical action of having to remove crystals, sorting out the alternatives and plugging them in takes consideration, and it is more likely to result in the checking of other users and the fitting of a new frequency pennant.

It may be queried why we cannot use any frequency, such as over the same spectrum used by domestic radio transmitters and receivers. It is simply because we are transmitting signals as well as receiving them, and chaos would reign if there were not international legislation governing the wavebands for specific uses. Obviously the military, ambulance services, coast guards, civil aviation, hospitals, taxis and a host of other organisations have radio frequency needs – and our hobby, in real terms, is not one of the most essential users. At least, not in the eyes of the bureaucrats.

## Operating ranges

For similar reasons we have a strict limit on the transmission output strengths from our transmitters. This in turn limits the range of our equipment, the distance between the transmitter and the model where safe operation is attained. This will vary between surface-borne and airborne models, the latter having a greater range than those operated on the ground or water. It may seem that the range is unnecessarily limited, but this is actually working to the benefit of the modeller. If, for instance, the equipment had a potential air range of 80 km (50 miles), there would be the risk of one modeller's equipment within that range interfering with that of another when operating on the same frequency. It is only possible to check on the frequencies being used by modellers on your particular model site – if you had to travel around a wide radius to ascertain the operation of other modellers, you would never have time to carry out your own modelling.

Modern radio control equipment has an airborne range of at least a mile (1.6 km), and this is about the optimum, particularly in highly populated countries. Most R/C modellers operate within groups or clubs, and it is not difficult for these organisations to ensure that they have a safe operating distance between the sites. For this reason it is important that modellers from all disciplines co-operate, as it may be that some common frequencies will be used.

From a visual point of view the range limitations are not a disadvantage. Large model ships and yachts are unlikely to go beyond the radio range, cars being raced keep within a short radius of the operators, and even the largest model aeroplanes begin to look small at a distance of 1 km.

## Frequency allocations

In the early days of radio control modelling, an allocation was given on the 27MHz band, and this had to suffice for all types of models. Because of the electronic limitations of the equipment the 'spot' frequencies were initially set at 50KHz separations, reducing to 25KHz spacings as equipment improved. For ease of identification of the frequency pennants that were affixed to the transmitter aerials, the spot colours were given specific colours; for example, 26.995MHz was brown, 27.045 red, 27.095 orange, and so on. With the subdivision of the 50KHz spots to 25KHz, the pennants of intermediate frequencies were designated by two colours, so 27.020 would be given a brown/red pennant.

With the onset of CB (Citizen's Band) radios using 27MHz frequencies, there came many problems resulting from interference of models from the CB outfits. In many cases the use of the CB radios on 27MHz was illegal, although oddly enough the purchase of the equipment was not illegal. To add to the problems,

CB'ers commonly boosted their signal output beyond the maximum permitted output of 4 watts. This would all be academic except that some radio equipment is still sold on 27MHz frequencies, and there may still be countries where it is the legal frequency for radio control models. Fortunately the craze for fitting CB to cars and lorries has greatly declined (the portable telephone being the 'in thing' at the moment), and the risk of interference from CB operators is therefore much less than it was. Even through the 'bad years' I continued to use 27MHz radio on our, admittedly reasonably remote, site and suffered no apparent instances of interference. However, on the grounds of safety it is recommended that 27MHz equipment is not used for model aircraft, and only used on surface vehicles with caution.

Many of the 'toy' R/C products are designed to operate on the 27MHz wave band, plus some other distinctly 'odd' frequencies, but the radiated output from these transmitters is so low as to be of no threat to the serious modeller – unless they are in very close proximity.

Radio regulatory boards in many countries have made separate allocations of wavebands for surface vehicles and aeroplanes. Thus boats, cars and other land and water vehicles will have one waveband, while aviators will have another allocation, sometimes more than one. This is obviously a sensible arrangement, as it allows the different disciplines to operate in close proximity to one another, knowing that there is no fear of co-interference. Perhaps this is not a serious problem under normal circumstances, but at public displays, where demonstrations of all types of R/C models may be

given, the need for frequency band separation is all-important. In these instances it is necessary for the common users of the surface vehicle frequencies to come to some accommodation, either by splitting the frequency allocation or by time periods. Boat users are often kind enough to operate on 27MHz, and at least their models are operating at very close range and are not moving at high speeds (except for racing classes). I am not suggesting that model boats are less superior as models, far from it, for they represent some of the highest standards of craftsmanship in any field.

Governing bodies of aeromodelling may try to encourage the use of specific spot frequencies for certain disciplines, for example power flyers using one range of 'spots', glider flyers another and helicopter operators a further number of spot frequencies. This, however, is a purely national arrangement and not one issued or governed by the international bodies.

Probably the most popular frequency bands in use throughout the world are the 35MHz band for aircraft (35.000 to 35.250MHz subdivided into 10KHz 'spot' frequencies) and the 40MHz band for surface vehicles (40.665 to 40.995MHz, again split into 10KHz 'spots'). Regrettably these band allocations are by no means universal, and many countries will have alternative bands allocated for modelling purposes. It is vital that, as an R/C modeller, you keep strictly to the legal frequencies provided by the government. The consequences of using illegal frequencies could be quite dire, resulting in interference with, for instance, hospital services and, from the other standpoint, the loss of your model. It is also important not to use an aircraft-designated

*The transmitter aerial should be fitted with a clearly visible frequency flag, appropriate to the frequency being used.*

frequency band for surface vehicles and vice versa, as this could also cause unnecessary interference between R/C models.

Modellers often avoid the risk of having two transmitters operating on the same frequency by using a pegboard system. Although the actual method of operation may vary from country to country, the principle remains the same. Before operating the transmitter the modeller must ensure that the frequency peg to match his operating frequency is displayed. It may be that the frequency peg is taken from the pegboard and placed on the transmitter, or the reverse may be true. Whatever the system in operation, it is the modeller's responsibility to understand it and to abide by it. A further check may be made by observing the frequency pennants displayed on the transmitters.

I have mentioned frequency pennants earlier in the chapter and these are our instant visual means of recognising the operating frequency of any specific

transmitter. It has been noted that they are colour coded, but they are also number coded. 40MHz equipment will have a green background and a number printed on the pennant; for example, 40.715MHz will be a green pennant over-printed with '715'. The background colour for 35MHz is orange and the numbers are in white; 35.030 will have a pennant number of 63.

In addition to the VHF bands (27, 35, 40MHz, etc), in certain countries, but principally the UK, there may be an apportionment on the UHF (Ultra High Frequency) band for R/C modellers. An advantage of UHF equipment is the reduced risk of interference; virtually the only risk is from a fellow modeller on the same UHF frequency, highly unlikely as few R/C sets have been sold on these frequencies. Using this frequency band, 458.5-459.5MHz, was of particular value when CB was interfering with the 27MHz band and before the additional frequency allocations for modellers. Against this advantage

of the UHF equipment must be set the additional cost of the equipment, because of the more complex electronics and higher component count. Also, because its use is not permitted in all countries, the major R/C equipment manufacturers have been reluctant to get involved in the manufacture of such equipment.

## Signal transmission

AM (Amplitude Modulation) equipment is not widely used today and is mainly confined to 27 and 40MHz frequencies for surface vehicles; this is at the lower end of the cost scale and often limited to two-function outfits. As the name suggests, the information is transmitted by a variation of pulse amplitude, something akin to varying the flow of liquid in a tap or valve. FM (Frequency Modulation) has already been mentioned, but virtually all 'top of the range' R/C outfits use PCM (Pulse Code Modulation) as the means for transmitting information to the receiver.

Before describing the operation of PCM it should be pointed out that an FM outfit cannot be operated on the same frequency as a PCM – or AM – transmission; it is only the method of transmission that varies, the frequency remains critical. Many of the PCM transmitters can also operate on FM (often referred to as PPM), and the equipment will specify if this is the case. The advantage with having dual PCM/FM transmission facilities is that the transmitter will operate with previously purchased FM receivers, which will not be obsolete, although having fewer functions. FM receivers tend to be less expensive than the PCM types.

## Pulse Code Modulation

When first mooted and before PCM became commercially available for the modeller, it was thought that it might allow all modellers to have their own individual frequencies, and that frequency control, pennants and pegs would become a thing of the past. Ten years later we are no nearer reaching this theoretical aim, and although the synthesised frequency systems are becoming available, the individual frequency side of the concept remains a dream. Even the dialled synthesised frequency is giving cause for concern, and the International Commission for Model Flying has issued a warning to avoid the switching on of transmitters without having verified the frequency:

'The transmitter frequency must be displayed on the outside of the transmitter or plug-in module or frequency switch. Also, frequency synthesised transmitters must be designed to display or change the programmed frequency prior to and without Radiated Frequency transmission.'

Perhaps we were getting the technology of the industrial world confused with the modelling applications where size, convenience *and* cost are paramount. There is little point in designing a system that will give us virtual total interference rejection if the transmitter has to be console based and the receiver weighs a few kilograms and measures half a cubic metre. Our modelling PCM may be less sophisticated than other systems, but it works and it is affordable.

At some time in the future it may be possible to develop synthesised frequency equipment that, before transmitting signals, will scan the frequency spectrum being used, note the 'spot' frequencies being operated and move to a vacant frequency; it will have to change the transmitter and receiver frequency *automatically* to the vacant 'spot'. Until this is achievable, and affordable, we will have to be vigilant in making frequency changes.

With the previous methods of transmission, AM and FM, we had the carrier signal that was altered in volume or frequency respectively. In theory, the AM system is more prone to interference in the 'quiet' parts of the transmission, whereas the FM signal is at a constant strength and therefore less likely to be affected by external interference. From personal observation, when an AM and an FM radio-equipped model were airborne together on the same frequency, I was not convinced that the theory was matched in practice, as the AM radio 'twitched' through the interference and never completely lost the signal. The model with the FM radio lost signal and crashed.

However, there were other reasons for dropping the use of AM transmission in radio control equipment. To achieve the high standards required for aircraft, fast boats and cars, plus the increased number of functions, the labour content in setting up the transmitter and receiver and the component count out-priced the FM outfits.

Pulse Code Modulation was made possible by the introduction of microprocessors, and as these have been developed over the years, so it has been possible to increase the number of functions programmable on the PCM transmitter and to improve the speed and accuracy of the data transmitted to the receiver, and from the receiver to the servos. Although operating digitally, the PCM signal is transmitted by the binary system using a code composed only of the numbers '0' or '1'. The receiver only has to detect an 'on' or 'off' situation and is less prone to interference; also, because of the super-speed of the micro-computer, it not only transmits the combinations of '1s' and '0s' in nano-seconds, but also has ample memory capability to decipher the code and to check for interference. The latter process involves checking whether the 'off' signals are totally clear, comparing them with previous 'frames' of signal, and deciding whether there is sufficient interference to warrant switching off the signal from the receiver to the servos. If the receiver decoder decides that the signals are obviously spurious, then it will go into a 'fail-safe' mode. The transmitter can normally be programmed so that the 'fail-safe' retains the servo positions in accordance with the last true signals, or moves them to a predetermined setting – for example, moving the throttle servo to cut the engine.

Whereas the AM and, to a lesser extent, the FM systems produced 'glitching' (with control alternating between 'on' and 'off'), which is frequently visible as the model moves erratically, the PCM equipment will give full control – or nothing. On receipt of interference the receiver will, once it has determined that a major signal problem has occurred, switch into the fail-safe mode and only return to normal operation when the interference has disappeared and a short delay has occurred. The delays, perhaps half a second, before switching in and out of fail-safe are there to confirm the situation and to prevent an oscillation of 'on' and 'off' that could be caused by intermittent interference.

For the R/C aircraft enthusiast, more so than surface vehicle operators, the model going into fail-safe is of great concern, and it can be frustrating to stand with a transmitter that is having no influence on the flight pattern of the model. It is, however, important to realise that with a non-PCM outfit there could have been a number of previous occasions when the model might have crashed through interference. The PCM system, by only cutting out when the interference has reached an intolerable level, may well have maintained operation when other systems would have failed.

Such is the speed of transmitting and decoding information that we can now take advantage of using faster and more accurate servos. The latest are more responsive and have smaller, or zero, 'deadbands' to take advantage of the improved data transmission technology – but more on that later.

As AM outfits have gradually been phased out in favour of FM, so probably will PCM be introduced at the basic levels of R/C outfits in favour of FM – until an even superior method of radio signal transmission is devised.

## PCM summary

1  PCM is only a different method of transmitting the data from the transmitter; it uses the same frequencies as AM and FM equipment. Therefore you cannot operate PCM equipment on the same frequency and at the same time as AM and FM outfits.

2  PCM is not interference-proof, but because of its internal checking system it is less likely to be affected by external interference.

3  The microprocessor is used not only for the decoding of signals but is also involved in a wide variety of mixing, rate switching, servo movement limiting, timing, low battery state and numerous other functions that were not previously available on FM systems.

*Economy two-channel radio control systems are well presented, and initial costs are minimised by the use of dry batteries. Re-chargeable nickel cadmium cells are an optional, and sensible, alternative.*

4  'Fail-safe' is a poor description for the 'lock-off' from the signal, and should be considered only as setting the servos to given positions. For virtually all types of models except gliders and yachts, the essential 'fail-safe' movement is to cut out the engine (things will

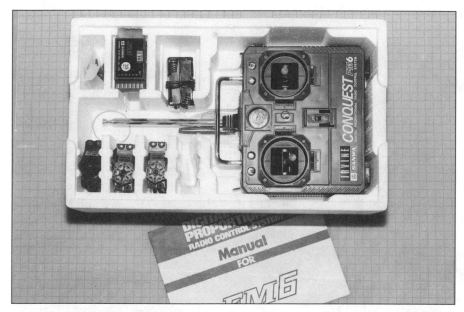 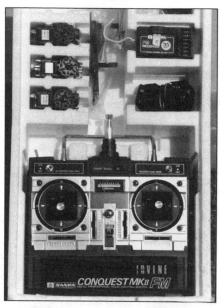

*Styling changes from the Sanwa 'Conquest' FM6 to the current MKII are seen here. The outfit can be purchased for dry battery operation with three servos, or fully nicaded and four servos.*

then happen more slowly and with less danger). How the remaining controls are set is a matter of conjecture; for an aeroplane it is probably safest to crash the model in the shortest distance possible.

## The component parts

Radio control equipment is sold, initially at least, as an outfit, and the typical basic items will consist of:
1  Transmitter
2  Receiver
3  Servos
4  Airborne battery pack and switch
5  Charger
6  Instruction booklet

At later stages certain items will be required separately, and manufacturers make provision for supplying these. Most modellers will want to have more than one model for operation and it may be inconvenient to remove and re-install servos, batteries and even the receiver. The original transmitter will almost certainly be suitable for operating more than one model, and there is no point in

purchasing a completely new outfit for a second or third model – although the method of costing may dictate that not a lot of money is saved when the servos, battery, receiver and switch harness are purchased separately. It is worthwhile comparing the total cost of buying the items that you require with the cost of a complete outfit, particularly bearing in mind that you are more likely to purchase the latter at a discount.

The following descriptions of the component parts are general and more related to the purchase of equipment than its precise function. There are differences in transmitters used for fixed-wing aeroplanes, helicopters and cars, and these specifics are dealt with in the chapters on the different disciplines.

## Transmitter

All transmitters are designed to be hand-held, even if some are supported in a tray, and within limits are of consistent size. They may vary in styling and detail

design, but they cannot vary to a great degree because the size of the hand determines the parameters of the design. The 'average' hand must be capable of reaching the control sticks and all the control switches, knobs, slides and buttons. Too small and it becomes cramped for the hands to locate and operate these controls, too large and the hands cannot reach all of the controls, and the transmitter becomes too heavy and unwieldy.

Manufacturers may talk of ergonomic design but the transmitter remains a basic oblong with the edges rounded off. It may have a tilted top section, it may have the aerial protruding at a different angle, but the degree of styling that the designer can incorporate is strictly limited. Like the family car, if different manufacturers put all the requirements through a computer, it will come up with similar designs, but there is still some room for selectivity.

As with a gun, fishing rod or tennis racket, the balance of the

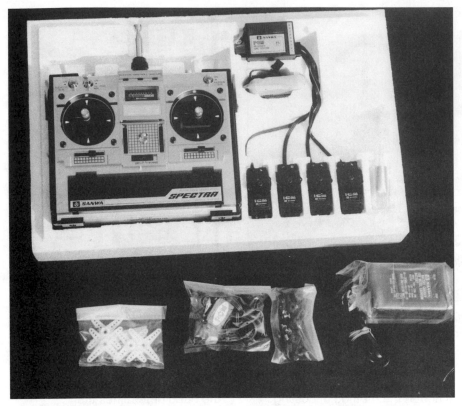

*More drastic styling changes have been applied to the Sanwa PCM outfits, from their previous 'Spectra' system to the later 'Exzes' and 'Infinity' transmitters.*

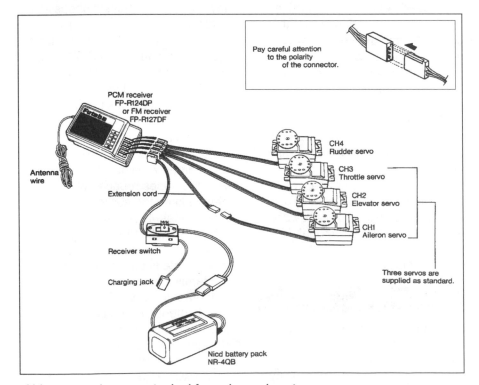

*Airborne package – a typical four-channel system.*

transmitter must be right. Again, this is more important if it is to be hand-held as opposed to having it fitted in a tray. The balance must, of course, be checked with the aerial extended, and at the same time the feel of the control sticks and location of the ancillary controls noted.

There are two common ways of controlling the transmitter sticks. The first is to support the transmitter with the flat of the hands and to rest the thumb on top of the sticks. Other modellers prefer to hold the sticks between thumb and forefinger, but with this method it may not be possible to support the weight of the transmitter on the little fingers, and it is then necessary to resort to the extra support of a neck strap or

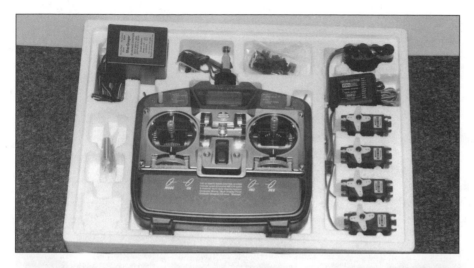

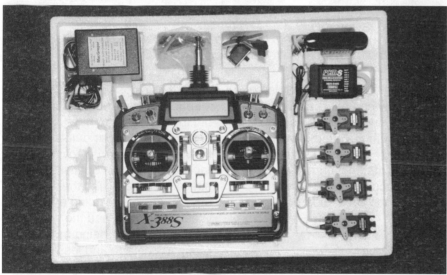

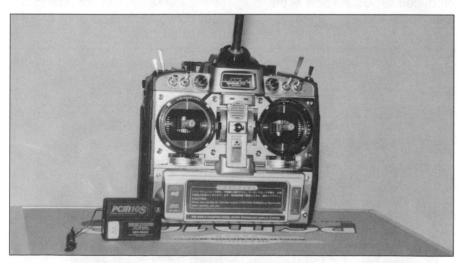

*Warning – radio control outfits can be seductive! Think carefully and buy the system most suited to your needs. JR computer outfits range from entry level to exotic, and FM non-computer from basic two-function to six channels.*

transmitter tray. A strap will simply take away the majority of the transmitter weight – the base of the transmitter is normally rested on the lower chest – while a tray allows the hands to be removed from all but the control sticks. Many experienced pilots maintain that a greater degree of precision can be achieved with the transmitter tray system, although this was not confirmed in recent World Championship results. In the helicopter and aerobatic aeroplane classes, probably requiring more precision than any other disciplines, three out of four of the top pilots chose to have hand-held transmitters. Another contentious aspect is the 'mode' of the transmitter, and we will return to this argument later.

## Receiver

Receivers will obviously match the transmission method of the transmitter – FM or PCM, for example – and will vary in the number of functions they provide. Simple two-function outfits will be totally designed for the dual functions to keep the costs to a minimum, but the more extensive equipment will have anything from four to ten functions. In many instances the printed circuit board, integrated circuits and electronics are identical irrespective of the number of functions being indicated, with only the number of servo sockets varying. The comparative price of the receivers does not always reflect their similarity.

Modern receivers are, from a practical standpoint, acceptably small and will fit into nearly all models of normal size without any problems. It is only when we wish to operate ultra-small models that subminiature receivers are required, and these are more likely

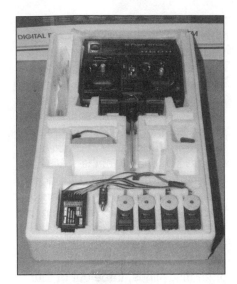

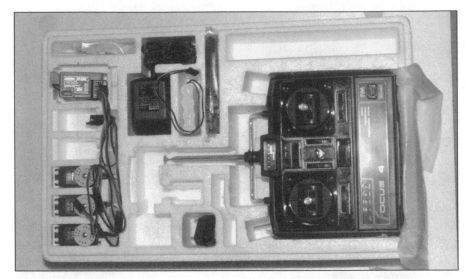

*Hitec equipment, made in Korea, is rapidly becoming a major force in the electronics industry. Separate car, fixed-wing aircraft and helicopter outfits are produced by them in both FM and computer PCM.*

to be available on FM equipment. Remember that the plugs and sockets, and probably the crystal, will have to remain at the same physical dimensions, so there is a limit to the sub-miniaturisation that can be achieved without it becoming highly specialised.

Receiver cases are made from tough plastic, designed to protect the electronics in all but the worst accidents and capable of withstanding the occasional fuel spillage. They are not waterproof, so if they are to be used in a wet environment they must be adequately protected.

Servos are connected to the receiver via plug housings in the terminal block, and the same applies to the power (battery) source; battery and servo numbers are indicated on the receiver case. The single loose wire is the aerial, and in no circumstances should this be strained or cut short. Equally, it must not be left in its wound-up state, and has to be located in a suitable position on the model – more of that later.

Provision will be made on the receiver for changing the crystal to one or another frequency. The crystal will probably be protected by a small rubber or plastic cover on the case; when this is removed

it exposes the crystal, which is removed by carefully pulling on the frequency number tab. It is then replaced with the alternative crystal, on the same frequency as the transmitter, ensuring that it is housed securely in the crystal holder on the circuit board.

## Servos

To my knowledge all commercially-produced servos are now of the rotary output types. For many

years it was possible to obtain alternative linear output servos, but these appear to have gone out of favour. The linear output servo had two output arms moving, by rack and pinion, in opposite directions. These had the advantages of providing a true linear movement and the disadvantages of being more prone to damage and less easy to adjust. Although not available as a complete servo, it is possible to buy conversions for changing

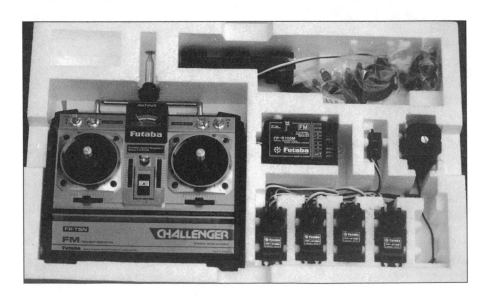

*Futaba are the largest manufacturers of radio control equipment and their highly successful 'Challenger' FM outfit (known as the 'Conquest' in some countries) has recently been superseded by the 'Skysport', with more mixing and adjustable functions. The 'Field Force 7' computer system is used throughout the world and appeals to all classes of radio control enthusiasts.*

rotaries to linear outputs. Perhaps the linear servo will make a come-back one day, although its benefits disappear if the control surface movement is itself through a rotary movement.

Another thing of the past, but which may be required for older sets, is an alternative rotation output servo. Every self-respecting modern transmitter, even the economy two-function outfits, have servo-reversing facilities so there is, theoretically, no requirement for having some servos operating in one direction and some in the opposite direction. However, before the days of servo-reversing this was almost essential, as some linkages, most notably to strip ailerons in aeroplanes, were very difficult to connect with a servo of the wrong rotation. I say 'theoretically' because there are still times when it is an advantage to have servo rotations of both directions.

For non-programmable transmitters, which are being used for more than one model, it will be necessary when changing from one model to another to operate servo-reversing switches to match the control movement requirements of the new model. If this can be avoided, and all the reversing switches left permanently in the same position, this eliminates another possible accident. I know of more than eight *truly* experienced R/C modellers who have crashed models through failing to check the servo-reversing switches correctly!

With the programmable PCM transmitters this problem no longer exists, as the servo-reversing positions are held on the memory for that particular model and will automatically be switched correctly when that model is called up. One tip, however – if you do need a servo to operate in the opposite direction from that supplied by the manufacturer, an alternative supply of servos, from a different maker but with the same plug, may have an opposite rotation output.

## Battery packs

The initial choice in batteries lies between the dry, alkaline, batteries of the type used in small torches, transistorised radios, toys, and so on, and the rechargeable nickel cadmium cells. Dry cells have only one redeeming feature – the initial cost is less. However, any serious R/C modeller would be well advised to forget about dry batteries; for one thing they are often discarded prematurely, simply because of the risk of them running down during operation. There is also the nuisance value of having to change the receiver batteries (often installed in the bowels of the model), while the battery boxes employed with dry batteries are rarely of the highest standard of reliability.

Nicads (nickel cadmium cells), used and charged correctly, can be recharged and recycled many hundreds of times and will give many years of service. Their reliability is as near to 100 per cent as you are likely to get, and any failure is likely to occur within the first few operations; it is sensible, therefore, to cycle the equipment three or four times before using it in a model. Simply charge the transmitter and receiver pack, switch on, operate the controls from time to time and check that all the servos are moving smoothly. This is also a wise precaution as a check on the components used in the equipment – weaknesses are likely to show up in the early stages of operation.

Nickel cadmium packs are available in a wide range of capacities and shapes, suited to all aspects of the hobby. For instance, the smallest of models may use 50 mAh nicads for the receiver/servo operation; these cells are exceptionally small but will give an operational time of 20-30 minutes when used with the correct receiver and servos. At the opposite end of the scale, large racing vehicles or boats and very large flying models can be fitted with 4000 mAh (4AH) battery packs.

The normal operating voltage of the receiver/servos is 4.8 volts, although this is sometimes boosted to 6 volts for larger models having

A. **Nylon Sealing Gasket**

B. **Resealing Safety Vent**

C. **Nickel Plated Steel Top Plate (Positive)**

D. **Positive Connector**

E. **Nickel Plated Steel Can (Negative)**

F. **Sintered Positive Electrode**

G. **Separator**

H. **Support**

I. **Sintered Negative Electrode**

J. **Negative Connector**

*The structure of a typical nickel cadmium cell.*

long leads between the receiver and servos and a consequent drop in voltage. Before going to the fifth cell for the receiver pack (nicad cells have a nominal voltage of 1.2v) you should always check that the receiver is designed to cope with the higher voltage. Transmitters are mostly designed to operate on 9.6 volts, and 600 mAh cells are most frequently used, although some sets will have the larger-capacity 1,000 to 1,200 mAh cells fitted.

Battery packs are usually fitted to the transmitter with a plug-and-socket attachment, but some of the economy sets may rely on a push-in, sprung battery box arrangement with the cells individually fitted. Both these and the types where a pack is sprung-contact-fitted should be checked from time to time and the contacts cleaned.

Virtually all of the nicad cells (except some 'button' cells) are capable of accepting rapid charging, certainly the case with those purchased through reputable

model dealers. However, it is rare that transmitters and receiver packs will require fast charging as it is usually carried out at the standard rate through the night prior to operating. There are, however, times when a switch has been accidentally left in the 'on' position, and in such cases a fast-charging facility is an advantage.

Nicads have improved substantially over recent years, and capacities for specific cell sizes have increased so that the typical pen cell, previously rated at 500 mAh, is now 600 mAh, and the Sub C cell at 1,200 mAh is now rated at 1,400 or even higher. The cells have also gone 'green', with the mercury content of their predecessors removed, while others use nickel metal hydride for better environmental considerations.

Fears have been expressed that nicad packs have a built-in 'memory', and that if a transmitter is charged regularly for the full 12/14 hours period but only used

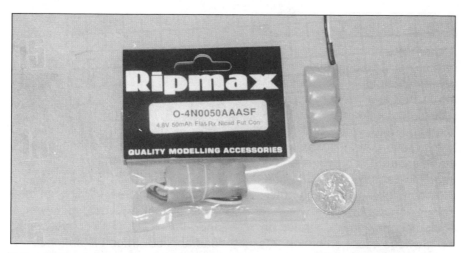

*Nicad battery packs are obtainable in a very wide range of outputs and sizes from tiny 50 mAh packs, and button cells are also used in some packs.*

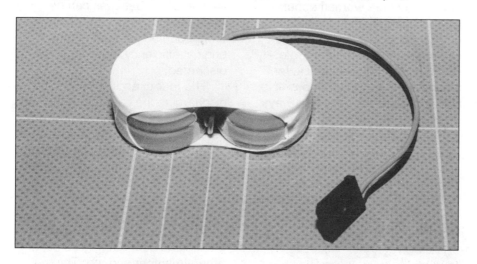

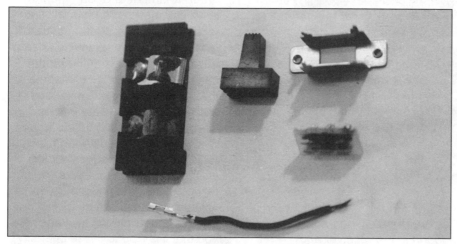

*'Black wire corrosion' is a little understood phenomenon, but does occur, and is shown here affecting the terminals in the transmitter battery box, the wire to the switch and the switch itself. When equipment is not being used the battery should be disconnected.*

each time for 30 minutes of operation, then when you wanted to use it for 90 minutes the batteries would lose voltage before the 90 minutes expired; this in spite of the transmitter having a normal operating time of, say, 120 minutes. However, these worries seem to have died down, and I have to admit that I have never experienced any proof that such a 'memory' ever existed – it never seemed to worry the military and industrial users.

There is one danger associated with the use of nicad packs, more so with the receiver batteries, and that is a phenomenon known as 'black wire corrosion'. In contrast to the 'memory theory', this is an actual occurrence and is to be found on the negative wire(s) between the battery pack and the switch. This negative wire corrodes and disintegrates to such an extent that there is a complete failure and no current can be passed through the wire. It is a gradual process, but fortunately one that does not seem to extend beyond the switch location to, for example, the receiver – and it is less likely, but not impossible, for it to be found in the transmitter negative battery wire.

Many theories have been put forward for this occurrence (including such unlikely ones as a different chemical being used for the black pigmentation of the wire covering), but the important fact is that it can happen and should be checked from time to time; it often occurs after about a two-year period. Disconnecting the battery from the switch will prevent this 'black wire corrosion' from happening, so if you are not using your model for some length of time, just unplug the battery. Direct wiring of the battery, via a switch or isolating socket, increases the risk of 'black wire corrosion' as the battery cannot be disconnected; in these circumstances the corrosion may reach the receiver. Military operators of nicad cell packs have been known to use a special nickel wire to overcome the corrosion problem, and it is to be hoped that R/C model manufacturers will follow suit.

New rechargeable battery developments are always welcome, the more so if they provide greater environmental acceptability and greater efficiency. The nickel metal hydride cells are only about two-thirds of the size of nicad cells of similar output, have no 'memory' effect, have a long service life (500-1,000 charge and discharge cycles), and are protected from polarity reversal. They are entirely suitable for transmitter and receiver packs, although less so for operating electric motors requiring a large current draw.

## Chargers

A charger is normally supplied as part of the radio control outfit. This has a dual output, one lead for the transmitter and one for the receiver pack, for charging at the 'standard' rate, ie one-tenth of the battery rating. At these rates the manufacturers will recommend a charging period of 14 to 16 hours (20 hours for the initial charge). This is done whether the equipment has been operated on the previous occasion or not. Modellers tend to become a little paranoid regarding the charging of nicads; they are worried about overcharging the battery and causing damage, or even an explosion. At this standard rate – 60 mAh for a 600 mAh pack, for example – it is virtually impossible to overcharge the cells, so always give a full charge before going

driving, flying or sailing. It is only with the fast charging that charging times are critical.

In addition to chargers it is possible to purchase cyclers, and these discharge the batteries to a nominal 1.1 volts per cell before fully charging them again. These certainly keep the batteries in good health, but the real advantage comes when there is a facility for checking the actual capacity of the pack. By making a note of the operational time (with an artificial load applied) when the batteries are new, a useful check on any deterioration throughout the lifetime of the batteries can be made. Once the batteries have dropped to 90 per cent of their original efficiency they should be discarded.

The fear of accidentally discharging the battery pack to the extent where it will fail applies particularly to airborne batteries. Where you are likely to be using the battery to its limits, and cannot fit one of larger amperage, it is prudent to fit a low voltage indicator. These small units contain a number of LEDs (light-emitting diodes) ranging from green to amber and red. The instructions with the units will tell you that when the lighting pattern reaches a certain stage it is unsafe to continue to operate the model. I can think of a number of models that could have been saved from crashes had these safety units been available at the time.

Transmitters are fitted with a radiated output or battery voltage indicator, and these will give you an immediate warning of reduced voltage. Many of the latest sets have an aural warning system to tell you that it is time to cease operating and to recharge the systems.

Nickel cadmium cells will stand

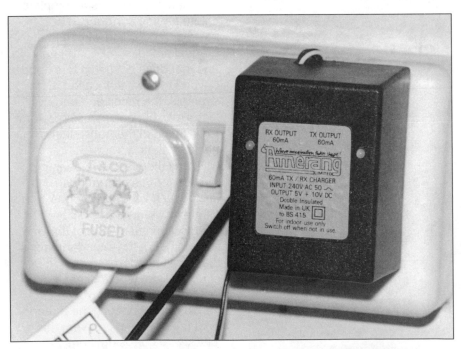

*Chargers supplied with radio control outfits are normally non-adjustable, fixed-output units with separate charging leads to the receiver and transmitter batteries. Designed to plug directly into a mains socket, they have small LEDs to indicate that charging is taking place.*

a considerable amount of abuse, but because they are so reliable they should not be taken for granted, and a little care and inspection should provide you with a number of years' usage.

## Instruction leaflet

The manufacturer has the problem of knowing just how much to include in his instructions, more normally in the form of a booklet than a leaflet. What I would prefer to see in the instructions is a general description of what the equipment does, a few hints on how to install it, how to operate it, what maintenance is required, and where to send it for repair and servicing (including information on packaging and insurance and what the guarantee covers). Most manufacturers provide adequate instructions, but there are certain problems. Because the modern computer sets have so many facilities – and the latest economy outfits not that many fewer – an enormous amount of the instructions space is taken up with information on how to programme this wide range of functions.

'User friendly' is an emotive term, but some of the earlier computer transmitters were anything but. Instruction books with over 100 pages of 'how to program' functions that even baffled the experts were not the way to go, and you needed a science degree to understand the systems and a day to spare before going out to 'gen up' on the workings.

In common with other consumer electronic goods, the R/C transmitter has been subjected to some radical thinking and redesign and now the programming and operation of the equipment is much more logical and easy to understand. However, the major percentage of the instructions do relate to the programming of functions, sometimes at the expense of the more basic descriptions of the complete outfit. To give an example, I recently read the owner's manual for a six-function FM computer outfit – a middle-of-the-range, programmable outfit. The manual commenced with a quick programme of basics to get you, in this case, airborne as soon as possible. When you wanted to learn more about specific features it referred you to the detailed programming information. In a 57-page booklet less than half a page was devoted to the installation of all the equipment, and no mention was made of how long the charging period should be, how to change the crystals or even what the plugs and sockets look like.

Perhaps it is because of these limitations that a book of the present description is needed; the outfit in question might well have been purchased by a newcomer to the hobby.

Distributors and Manufacturers to the Model Trade, TV and Film Industries
Manufacturers of Electronic and Insulating Components -
Radio Control Equipment.

**THE INSTALLATION AND OPERATION
OF MACGREGOR / JR
RADIO CONTROL SYSTEMS**

*MacGregor sensibly include their own instruction booklet to augment the imported JR outfits, covering general items of charging, frequency crystals, etc.*

# Chapter 2

# Heart of the Matter – the Transmitter

The transmitter is the controller of the radio control system. From this unit signals are sent to the receiver and passed on to the servos, which set the ailerons, or whatever, to the positions dictated by the transmitter operator. These are the raw facts, but the description of how this is achieved and the alternative methods involved is more complex, and the variety makes it impossible to give a single explanation. In the interests of clarity, therefore, the descriptions and information in this chapter will deal with aircraft transmitters, ie power models, gliders and helicopters. This is because the control requirements are greater in these disciplines than are needed in vehicles and boats, and there are more functions to consider and understand. Many of the comments will be equally applicable to the other aspects of our hobby, and where there are variations they will be dealt with in the chapters dealing with those activities.

## What mode?

Standardisation of R/C equipment was a little late in arriving, so we still have one or two anomalies. Switches are normally now positioned in the up position for 'on', but there are still a few where 'on' is down.

However, the most important variation concerns the functions of the two main control sticks on the transmitter, or the 'mode' layouts.

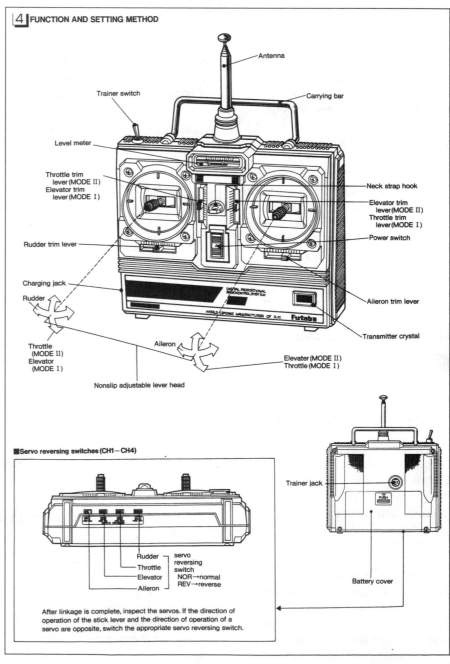

*Typical layout of a non-computerised FM transmitter. Note the directions of the transmitter sticks for the Mode 1 (I) and Mode 2 (II) arrangements.*

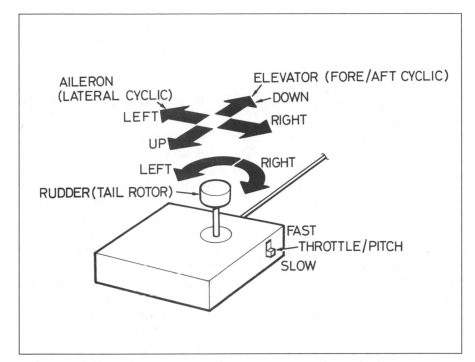

*Modes 3 and 4 are not frequently used, and there are few 'cuddle box' (Mode 3) transmitters commercially available. Mode 4 may suit left-handed modellers and is the same arrangement as Mode 1, but with the aileron and rudder functions reversed.*

*Why Mode 3 is known as 'cuddle box'! Rudder control is on top of the single stick, and the throttle is operated by a slide switch at the side of the transmitter case.*

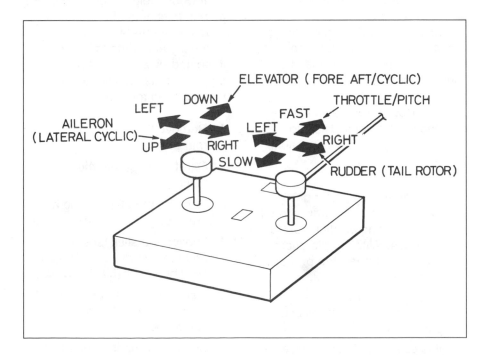

In Mode 1 the right-hand stick controls the ailerons (movement left and right) and the throttle (up and down). On the left-hand stick is the elevator (up and down) and the rudder (left and right). Mode 2 transposes the throttle and elevator functions so that the right-hand stick controls the elevator and aileron functions. These modes are often referred to as 'split sticks' for Mode 1, and 'single stick' for Mode 2; this is because the terms refer to the two primary controls, ie elevator and aileron (or, in the case of only three functions being used, rudder). A similar disparity is experienced by glider and helicopter pilots.

It was a great shame that when we moved from the non-proportional equipment, using two-action self-centring switches, to full proportional transmitters, with two control sticks, only one arrangement was manufactured. We are therefore blessed – or cursed – for the foreseeable future with the alternative layouts.

So which is the best arrangement? Ask a dozen different and experienced R/C modellers and you will find no unanimity. In truth, it is more related to where you began your R/C modelling career than to which mode is most suited to your manual dexterity. Certain countries, and certain areas within countries, adopted either Mode 1 or Mode 2 as their preferred system, and these divisions have tended to remain. As new modellers come along to clubs and are taught by local experienced flyers, it is obvious that they will be taught with the mode prevalent in that area. For this reason it is sensible, before purchasing equipment that cannot easily be converted from one mode to another, to check with local modellers or model shop to ascertain the mode common to the area.

This still does not answer the basic question of which, all other things being equal, is the best arrangement of the transmitter. Perhaps we should look at the champions and see how they perform. Again, however, there is no unanimity, suggesting that once you have learned to fly it does not matter too much whether you are flying 'single stick' or 'split sticks'.

It might be tempting to try to relate R/C operation with the flying of full-size aircraft. Forget that idea, however – having learned to fly full-size aircraft, piston-engined and jets, before flying R/C with proportional control, I can confirm that similarities are purely superficial. I even tried a transmitter with a twist knob on top of a single stick to attempt to emulate, as near as possible, the controls of a full-size aircraft. The fact that you are not sitting in the aircraft but having to watch from outside and, consequently, looking and then reacting, makes the two skills quite different. The same argument can, of course, be used for R/C cars. Eventually I came down on the side of Mode 1, ie with the ailerons on

the right and elevator on the left. Having taught quite a few modellers to fly and being able myself to fly on both modes, I believe Mode 1 has a slight edge on the 'single stick' arrangement for the following reasons.

Control sticks are electro-mechanical devices and the primary functions, plus rudder, have a self-centring arrangement. This is achieved by the use of springs, which have a linear movement, ie the stick will move more easily directly up and down or from side to side than it will towards the corners. Primary functions, in use for most of the time, are rarely in the centralised positions; conversely, the secondary functions, ie throttle and rudder, are used much less. Therefore 'split sticks' are keeping to the 'natural' self-centring axis most of the time, while with 'single stick' you are constantly 'battling' into the corners.

Most of the advantages of the 'split sticks' are related to the above factors, but they may be summarised as follows:

1 The less co-ordinated flyer or beginner is not so likely to make a mess of *two* functions at a time.

2 Left-handed people can co-ordinate on a standard 'split stick' transmitter without modifications or stick control changes. With 'single stick' they would need the primaries on the left-hand stick.

3 There is no unwanted interaction between roll and pitch axis.

4 It is easy to hold on precise amounts of elevator or aileron control at the moment of hand launch without having the possibility of disturbing the other primary function.

5 For certain aerobatics, where a fixed amount of one control (aileron or elevator) is required and slight corrections with the other primary, 'split sticks' must be an advantage.

Manufacturers seem at last to have accepted that the two different modes are here to stay, and they are now making provision on their programmable transmitters to operate on either Mode 1 or 2. The only action then required, apart from accessing the stick mode selection, is to change over the ratchet and spring arrangement for the non-centralising throttle movement. Aileron, elevator and rudder all move back, by spring-centring, to the neutral position, as determined on the transmitter, but the throttle position needs to remain at the set position until changed by the operator.

It would help the purchaser, if he has to change the mode, to have a diagram of the stick assembly and parts to be relocated. A written description only is not the easiest form of instruction to follow:

1 Remove the screws on the rear panel.

2 Carefully separate the two halves of the transmitter.

3 Remove the plate spring and brass stay from the control box.

4 Loosen the stick tension screw and remove the coil spring and coil spring bar (black plastic).

5 Install the brass stay and plate spring on the other side of control box.

6 Set the coil spring and plastic bar on the other side of the control box.

7 The mechanical conversion is now complete, so re-assemble your transmitter.

## Functions, features and flexibility

There is no such thing as the perfect R/C outfit, or the ultimate system. There are, however, outfits that are more suited to your particular needs than others. What those needs are only you can determine – they will depend on the types of models you are operating, their complexity, how many models you wish to operate from the same transmitter, and, equally importantly, how much money you are prepared to spend in pursuance of your hobby. Perhaps a reminder that it is a hobby and all about enjoyment and pleasure would not go amiss at this point. As I said before, we are not buying equipment for equipment's sake; we only need the standard sufficient to operate our present models and those of the foreseeable future. Trying to plan too far ahead is pointless as R/C equipment is constantly evolving and today's hi-tech may be tomorrow's dodo.

It is impossible to review all of the commercial R/C outfits in a manual such as this, so I am going to take a look at four typical outfits that cover the range from the economy sets to the most comprehensive of computerised PCM outfits, but first a word about channel/function terminology.

## Channel/function terminology

When non-proportional multi-channel equipment was the norm for radio control operation, the outfits were termed as having a certain number of channels. In these instances two channels would be used for one function, ie the elevator would have the switch operating 'up' for one channel and

in the opposite direction for the second channel. This form of designation is still used for R/C equipment in Germany; for instance, a Graupner C12 12-channel receiver will be operating six servos – or functions.

Modern proportional equipment, most of it being manufactured in the Far East, refers to the number of functions as channels. So a Sanwa Vanguard FM 4Ch, or a Digifleet four-channel XP/FM transmitter, will provide the means of controlling four control functions – in the case of an aeroplane, elevator, aileron, rudder and engine throttle.

The change of meaning of 'channel' has led to a confusing state of affairs, but any model shop proprietor with a knowledge of radio control will be able to advise you on any specific outfit. Using the term 'channel' to

indicate the number of functions is by far the most common present-day designation, so you will see the numbers 4, 5, 6, 7 and 8 (even 10 on the most advanced outfits) signifying the number of functions provided.

FM (Frequency Modulation) is also referred to as PPM (Pulse Position Modulation) – these terms have identical meanings.

## Four-channel outfit for aeroplanes, cars and boats

This outfit might be available on 35MHz and 40MHz (possibly other frequencies specific to particular countries), but it will not be suitable for helicopters, which require a minimum of five channels (functions).

Although dry batteries may be an option, it would be good economics to purchase in the first

*The basic four-channel transmitter does not have rate or mixing functions, but does include trims and a servo reversing facility.*

instance the all-nicad version with charger. A three- or six-month warranty will be included, but it is important to check that there is a servicing agent in your country – well over 90 per cent of all R/C outfits are produced in the Far East (Japan, Singapore, Korea and Hong Kong), so a local authorised servicing agent is important.

A low-cost outfit of this description will often be sold with only three servos, but this may be sufficient for the modeller just coming into the hobby, and the supplier has to make his equipment as cost competitive as possible. Additional servos are always readily available.

The main features of the outfit are as follows (for a fuller explanation of the features, see the subsequent section on nine- and ten-channel outfits):

## Transmitter

Four channels (functions), FM (PPM)
Gimbal sticks with adjustable length and tension
All-channel servo reversing
Adjustable travel volume (ATV) on all four channels (also known as 'end point adjustment' and 'travel adjustment')
Master/student ('buddy box') training system
Crystal change facility
Trims on all channels

## Receiver

Ultra narrow band width (frequency)
Dimensions: 37 x 61 x 22 mm
Weight: 45.5 g
Current drain: 22MA
Range quoted as 3000 feet (900 metres) in the air

## Servos

Oilite bearings
Indirect drive
Positive pulse width (1550 US/IN)

*On five- and six-channel standard transmitters the additional functions are usually switched by a lever or rotating knob on to top of the transmitter; there may also be a switch for the training system.*

Current drain: 8MA at 6 volts
Torque: 33.0 kg/cm (at the
output disc)
Speed: 0.21 seconds/60 degrees
Size: 41 x 20 x 36 mm
Weight: 43 g

You would have to buy the
outfit as a Mode 1 or Mode 2 set,
for although it would be possible to
change over the mechanics, the
servo reversing and ATV (or 'end
point') adjustment might then not
relate to the appropriate functions.

Missing from this outfit, which
might be found on a slightly more
expensive system, are rate
switches and mixing facilities.

## Six-channel FM computer system with ABC&W technology

Strangely, the manufacturer does
not explain what 'ABC&W
technology' is in his owner's
manual or advertising (it actually
means 'Anti-blocking, anti-cross
modulation and windows').

In their efforts to keep one step
ahead of their competitors, the
designers of radio control
equipment tend to improve the
specification standards of their
equipment within a given position
in the market. For not too much
more than the cost of an economy
outfit it is now possible to buy a
computer system, still FM but with
a two- or three-model memory and
many of the features that were
previously only to be found on the
high-cost outfits. The problem for
the manufacturers lies not in the
updating of the lower- and middle-
price equipment, but what can be
introduced on the upper-market
outfits. In effect it would seem that
the modeller has all the control
commands that he needs – until
the manufacturer persuades
him otherwise.

*Five- and six-channel FM (PPM) transmitters. The Max 66 can be programmed for fixed wing or helicopter aircraft and has a two-model memory. The programming of the Hitec Flash 5, for fixed wing only, is explained in Appendix 3.*

Helicopters and fixed-wing powered aircraft require some different controls, although the basic four functions are similar. The computerised systems can normally cope with this situation; it is just a matter of entering the system mode (not to be confused with the Mode 1 and Mode 2 stick arrangements) and select the model type.

## General features

Six channels (functions), FM
Two-model memory
Two model types (aircraft and helicopter)
Servo reverse on all channels
Travel volume adjustment
Sub-trim
Transmitter low battery alarm
Dual rates and variable travel response (soft centres)
Adjustable trims with positive centring
Interchangeable Mode 1 and Mode 2
Direct servo control (DSC)
Trainer system

The outfit would be supplied with transmitter, miniature receiver (using surface-mounted components), four servos, all nicads, switch harness, servo accessories and operating manual.

Aeroplane computer software
Flap/elevator compensation
Flaperon mix
V-tail mix
Aileron/rudder mix
Elevator/flap mix
Optional single-switch operation of both aileron and elevator rates

Helicopter computer software
Two three-point throttle curves (idle up)
Three three-point pitch curves
Throttle hold with pitch curve and rudder offset
Revo mix

Flight mode switch (changes the sensitivity of the throttle curve, pitch curve, dual rate and gyro sensitivity).

Again, the more obscure terms will be explained in more detail in a moment.

Transmitter
FM (PPM)
Power source: 9.6 volts (8 x 1.2v 600 matt nicads)
Output power: approximately 1 watt
Current drain: 200MA (giving a safe 2 hour operating period)

Functions are accessed by pressing two buttons (mode and channel) simultaneously; the LCD screen on the front of the transmitter will indicate a data reset function. The mode button is then pressed until the function required is indicated, then the channel button is pressed until the desired channel, for example elevator or throttle, comes on to the screen. If changes in the form

of percentage movement alterations are required, ie travel adjustments, mixing percentages etc, the 'increase' and 'decrease' buttons are pressed accordingly. When the model has been fully trimmed to the pilot's requirements, the settings are banked into the transmitter's memory. The memory options on this transmitter are one each of helicopter and aeroplane, or two of one type of model.

### Eight-channel PCM/PPM selectable, with eight-model memory for powered aeroplanes, gliders or helicopters

Although the description of this outfit refers to aircraft, it is also manufactured on the 40MHz band and is suitable for cars and boats. Some of the features may not be directly applicable to surface vehicles, but many operators of these craft will be looking for top-

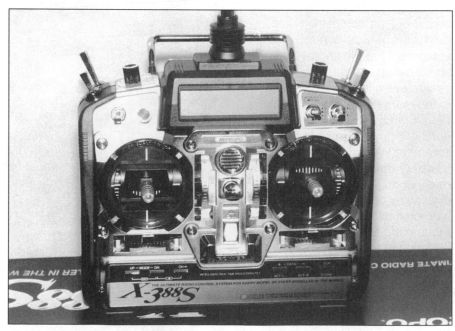

*JR Propo 388S refers to 3 items, 8 models, 8 channels and PCM/PPM selectable*

*Sevens and eights – all of these computerised transmitters (above and left) are PCM and, provided that they are used with PCM receivers, have a fail-safe facility. They may also be used with FM receivers. Available in Mode 1 or Mode 2 stick arrangements, the X-388S and FF7 are suitable for all types of models, the Prism 7 more specifically for fixed-wing aircraft.*

quality radio control equipment, and such facilities as fail-safes, easy programming and adjustments of controls, multi-model memory, etc, will appeal to them.

The principal difference between this and the two previous systems is in the method of transmitting the signal; this example has PCM (Pulse Code Modulation). In addition to offering more features, the PCM equipment is generally recognised as possessing superior interference rejection. The appearance of the transmitter may not be greatly different from the six-function unit; the LCD screen may be a little larger, but access to the computer program is still by buttons, two more of them. There will also be a few more switches and knobs on the transmitter surface.

## General features

Three model types (powered fixed-wing, glider and helicopter)
Eight-model memory, fully flexible for model type
Eight channels (functions) for complex models
Programming via press buttons and visual confirmation on LCD
Selectable modulation – PCM or PPM (FM)
Programmable fail-safe: servo 'freeze' or pre-determined fail-safe position for each function
Mode selection
Dual and exponential rates
Servo reverse on all functions
Electrical trims with positive centring on transmitter
Programmed sub-trim
Differential servo travel adjustment of up to 150 per cent
Trainer system on all or selected control functions
Timer functions with audible warnings
Direct servo control (DSC)

*Before the introduction of computerised transmitters, variations of control mixing, 'end point' adjustment, snap roll inputs and dual rate percentages were made with 'trim pot' rotations. Note the plug-in RF output module, useful if you wish to change to a different frequency band (not a 'spot' frequency within a band) to fly in a different country.*

## Specific features for fixed-wing aeroplanes

Elevator/flap mixing
Landing attitude programming
Snap roll
Differential aileron mixing
Flap value knob adjustment
Specific features for gliders
Elevator to flap mixing
Aileron to flap mixing
Differential aileron mixing
Flap to elevator mixing
'Butterfly' ('crow') mixing
Dual flap trim (four-servo wing programming)
Three-position camber switching

## Specific features for helicopters

Stunt trim
Swash adjuster
Throttle hold

Throttle curve
Pitch curve
Inverted flight switch
Revolution mixing
Acceleration mixing

**Nine- or ten-channel PCM computer system, available separately for fixed-wing or helicopters**

Advances in the design of radio control equipment come at such a rate that it is only possible to generalise on the features included in the highest-specification outfits. There will undoubtedly be additions between the time of writing this book and its publication; refer to Appendix 3 for some of the latest features to be introduced.

Because the nine- or ten-channel PCM/FM outfit has more features than the previous sets, the opportunity will be taken to describe their purpose in more detail.

### Transmitter

Micro-computer system employing a large, clearly visible LCD 'soft touch' panel display.
700mAh nicad battery, giving long safe operation (200MA current drain), is plug-in and can be changed easily.
Adjustable stick length and tension – some modellers require a softer feel to the stick movements
Central processing unit (CPU) allowing compatibility with the maximum number of receiver types, PCM and FM (PPM)
Memory capability for ten model settings; alternatively, one model can be given two or more different settings.
Five-year-life lithium back-up battery, preventing loss of the memory should the transmitter nicad be removed or go flat.
Fully swivelling, collapsible aerial stored in the transmitter case when not in use.

### Receiver

High-performance PCM/FM dual conversion (to prevent interference from transmitters in the low ranges of the frequency band interfering with those in the higher ranges) with 10KHz narrow band circuitry)
Central processing unit (CPU) providing high resistance to electro-mechanical noise (useful for helicopters and spark-ignition-powered models).
High signal selectivity for rejecting cross modulation from common transmission sources.
Low current consumption.
Small size and weight (21 x 53 x 38 mm, 45 g).
Gold-plated connectors for increased conductivity.

*Top-of-the-range ten-channel! Enough functions here to satisfy the most innovative modeller – indeed, you may struggle to think of ten different functions that you can incorporate in the model. They are PCM with a programmable multi-memory (virtually limitless in the case of the Futaba 1024Z), and with many switchable programmes during operation. With so many functions and options the transmitter case is inevitably festooned with switches, sliders and knobs. It is not impossible to operate all of them, but you will have to do your homework to avoid operating the wrong switch. Soft touch switches are provided for programming, and the LCDs are large and provide plenty of information. The initial cost of these 'combos' – servos are not usually supplied with them – is high, but it does include many facilities that would normally be thought of as 'optional' extras. Retract speed variation, landing attitude system, tachometer, servo testing and comprehensive mixing are incorporated in these outfits.*

## Servos

(Because of the complexity and relatively high cost of this type of equipment it is often sold as a 'combo', ie with transmitter and receiver only).

Dual ball-bearing output capable of enduring high-vibration. environments (powered aircraft, IC powered cars, etc).

High-resolution, precise neutral positioning, zero deadband and smoothness of mechanical operation.

High-torque coreless motor and indirect drive feedback potentio-meter for better vibration protection. Dust and moisture resistant. Low current drain.

## Special features – fixed-wing aeroplane outfit

### Base-loaded active antenna

An alternative short, soft, plastic-covered, flexible base-loaded transmitter aerial (sometimes referred to as a 'rubber duck' aerial) is available.

### Direct servo control

DSC enables you to make adjustments to your model without transmitting any RF (radio frequency). The main transmitter switch is left in the 'off' position, and by plugging the DSC lead into the transmitter socket at one end and the receiver charging plug at the other, all normal function adjustments can be made, and the LCD display will be lit.

### Touch panel operation

Just touch the key portion displayed on the LCD screen and a bleeping sound will confirm the input. The plus and minus adjustment functions have an automatic repeat function with the finger pressure maintained, while small individual movements are also possible by single touches.

## Battery alarm

When the transmitter voltage drops below a set figure (9.0v) the display will flash the word BATTERY and simultaneously an audible alarm will sound four times. After a pause the alarm will again sound four times. If the model is being operated at the time of the warning, it should be retrieved as soon as possible.

## Back-up battery

The lithium battery has a five-year life and will protect the model memories in the event of a transmitter nicad failure. When the lithium battery eventually fails, the display will indicate this failure, again also with an audible alarm, and the battery must be replaced. This must only be done by an approved Service Agent, as extensive damage could occur if you attempt it yourself. With the end of the life of the lithium back-up battery you will also lose the memory settings for the models programmed in the transmitter. For this reason it is recommended that you fill in data sheets, listing the settings for each aeroplane; these can then be re-programmed when the transmitter has been re-batteried.

## Switch position warning

If any switches that could be dangerous are in the 'on' position (the landing attitude switch, for example) there will be an audible warning and the display will indicate the source of the potential danger.

## Data input

Two methods of entering data into the transmitter are available, the Direct Mode and the Code Number Access.

For the Direct Mode the codes are called up on the screen in turn until the function you require is

*The LCD layout on the Futaba PCM T9Z display indicates the model number, type of transmission (PCM), actual time, transmitter voltage and trim status. The soft key Q is pressed to call up the System Menu, then the appropriate key from A to R will take you into the particular function o be programmed.*

available and highlighted. Adjustments are then made before the original screen is restored and you move on to the next function and adjustment.

For Code Number Access the functions are all coded (for example, the 'modulation' selection might be '64'); the number is pressed on the LCD screen (function mode), which will call up the required function and the adjustments can then be made. It is a quicker system, but you must remember the code numbers or refer to the owner's manual.

## Reversing switches

This is an electronic means of reversing the throw (rotation) of any of the servo functions. The screen will indicate the position of all servo positions, ie normal or reverse, and they can be changed accordingly. By having this facility the servos can be fitted into the model without having to consider the direction of travel.

## Adjustable travel volume (ATV) or 'end point adjustment'/'travel adjustment'

This feature is used to achieve the proper servo throw and to prevent the servo from stalling as a result of the movement of the control reaching its limit. A stalled servo can quickly drain the receiver (or servo) battery pack and also cause damage to the servo. The travel adjustment range is typically 0-150 per cent (1-60 degrees) from the neutral or centre position, and can be adjusted individually for each direction.

## Throttle ALT

This function makes the throttle stick trim active only when the throttle stick is less than halfway down, ie set at less than half throttle. This provides for accurate idle adjustments without affecting the high throttle position. It is operative only on the throttle control.

## Dual rate/exponential adjustments

Dual rate and exponential adjustments are available on the three basic controls of aileron, elevator and rudder, with exponential also being offered on the throttle function. Having two rate positions allows you at the flick of a switch to increase or decrease the sensitivity of a control function. At the higher rate there will be a greater travel of the servo output, consequently giving more control surface movement and greater sensitivity of the control. Low rate will give a reduced sensitivity of control and may be switched in when smooth flying is required between the take-off and landing aspects of the flight, or during aerobatics.

Exponential control reduces the sensitivity around the neutral, progressively increasing the control effectiveness as the stick is moved to its maximum position. With the normal stick control the servo responds in a linear manner throughout its full movement. It is possible to change this to a full exponential movement – as described before – as a combination of exponential travel followed by linear movement (or the reverse), or to set the movement on VTR (variable trace rate). VTR is in effect a combined rate system where the initial part of the servo movement is at the lower rate, then, at a predetermined point, moves into the higher rate. To offer further variations (and possibly to confuse), there is also the choice of linear/exponential, or exponential/linear movement of the two rates. It is difficult to imagine what this system has to offer the model pilot over the exponential and dual rate operations, and it would be a brave flyer who could swear that he recognised the system without knowing that the transmitter had been so programmed.

## Sub-trim adjustment

The sub-trim adjustment is a feature that enables you to fine-tune the servo centres electronically by allowing you to select the centre, or neutral, of the servo with the mechanical trim tab at the centre position. Therefore any model called up on the transmitter will have the correct trim settings with the trim tabs at their centre location. (It is, of course, possible to adjust the control surfaces on the model to achieve the same purpose.)

---

## Adjustable Travel Volume/ End Point Adjustment

The purpose of adjustable travel volume (ATV), also known as end point adjustment, is to offer you precise servo control deflection in either direction of servo operation. The PCM-10S offers ATV for all ten (10) channels. The travel adjustment range is from 0% to 150% (0-60 degrees) from neutral, or center, and can be adjusted for each direction individually.

### Accessing and Utilizing the ATV or End Point Adjustment

To access the adjustable travel volume, enter Code 12 in the code number access selection or use the direct mode method.

The screen will appear as follows:

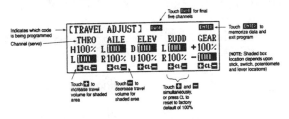

Use this feature to achieve the proper servo throw and to keep the servo from binding. A servo that has stalled can quickly drain the receiver battery pack and become damaged in the process.

To adjust the travel volume, move the appropriate control stick (lever, switch, potentiometer) to the right or left of center to the direction of travel you want to adjust.

*Note: The shaded box follows whichever direction you move the control. It is this value that you will be adjusting.*

Press the + key to increase the amount of servo travel and the - key to shorten the amount of servo throw. If you want to reset the travel throw to the factory default, 100%, you can either press the + and - keys simultaneously or press the CL key.

After adjusting the travel volume for all ten (10) channels, press the ENTER key to exit this function and memorize these values.

---

*An extract from the instruction manual for the JR PCM-10S outfit, explaining the programming for ATV and giving an example of the screen display.*

## Cross-trim

Mechanical trims on the transmitter are located adjacent to the control stick of the same function; thus the elevator trim is inboard of, and adjacent to, the elevator stick, moving vertically. Activation of the cross-trim electronically transposes these trim controls. It may be that numerous elevator trim changes may be needed during the flight of a particular model, and it may be more convenient to use the opposite hand for these mechanical adjustments, leaving the other hand permanently on the elevator stick.

## Flap

When activated, the flap lever raises or lowers the flaps in unison. In the lowered position the flaps reduce the stalling speed of the model and increase the lift.

## Auxiliary 3

This can be used to droop or raise the whole of the trailing edge of the wing, in unison with the flap movement. Although of little application to powered models, it has distinct advantages in competition sailplane work. Raising the wing trailing edge, to give the lowest drag coefficient, can be used for the 'speed' runs. The opposite movements may be equally advantageous when maximum lift is required for the duration element of the contest. In place of a completely moving trailing edge, the ailerons can be programmed, via Aux 3, to move in unison with the flaps, ie when the flaps are lowered the ailerons are also drooped, but to a lesser degree. Control movements combining flaps/moving trailing edge/ailerons should be made in very small increments, and the results noted before increasing the

movements. Using a programmable LCD display touch panel with many options makes the gradual introduction of changes very easy.

## Auxiliary 4 – Crow mixing

Rotating the Aux 4 knob lowers or raises the inboard flaps at the same time as moving the ailerons in the opposite direction. This is commonly known amongst the glider fraternity as 'butterfly' or 'crow' mixing. When operated to its full extent the drag increase is dramatic, and it is a particularly useful function for achieving accurate spot landings. It may be necessary to counter a downward pitching change of trim with some 'up' elevator control on the transmitter stick, and the aileron response may be lessened.

## Auxiliary 5

The Aux 5 knob, when activated, raises one flap while simultaneously lowering the opposite one. Used in conjunction with the ailerons it will produce a higher rate of turn – at the expense of a little efficiency.

## Variable pitch propeller mixing

Variable pitch propellers were popular in aerobatic contests for a short while, but they have now gone out of favour; they would be a useful control for large and heavy scale models. Ideally, propeller pitch would be operated as a separate function, but because we have a limited number of hands to control the transmitter, it is mixed with throttle control. As the throttle is advanced, the propeller moves into coarse pitch, but it is also possible to program a time delay so that, during take-off for instance, the propeller remains in fine pitch for up to one second

before moving into coarse pitch. It is also possible to select the throttle position at which the propeller pitch change occurs. The function can be switched on or off during flight.

## Wing type selection – 'flaperons'

'Flaperons' allow the pilot to use the existing ailerons also as flaps. Although it is possible to program the ailerons to move upwards as well as downwards, it is the latter position that is likely to be the most useful. Differential rate may be introduced to limit the amount of the down-moving aileron and increase the up-moving aileron in proportion. This reduces the risk of unwanted yaw caused by the additional drag of the aileron in the higher pressure air on the wing underside. As with many of these adjustable functions, experiment-ation is the only way of finding out the optimum amounts of flap input and degree of differential.

## Wing type selection – 'elevons'

Flying-wing and delta-wing designs will frequently use 'elevons' to control the lateral (roll) and longitudinal (pitch) control of the aeroplane; combining the elevator movements together (pitch) or in opposition to one another (roll) gives the elevon its name – elevator and aileron. As with the flaperons, the travel volumes, dual rates, sub-trims and differential are all adjustable on the servos operating them on each side.

## Quad flaps

A variety of input functions is available with the quad flap arrangement. Most importantly, for the contest glider enthusiast, it allows the effective camber of the wing section to be changed, providing more lift or more speed. It is also possible to utilise the inner wing trimmable panels as flaps and the outboard pair as ailerons. As the name suggests, the four panels (think of them as flaps and ailerons) are individually controlled by servos, and this allows full mixing facilities as mentioned previously under Cross-trims or Flap, Aux 3, Aux 4 and Aux 5.

## V-tail mixing (also called 'ruddervator')

In the V-tail control the elevator and rudder servos are mixed so that they can both operate in unison, as an elevator, or in opposition to one another, to behave in the rudder mode. Travel adjustments are available, as are dual rates and sub-trims, but there are limits of 75 per cent of the normal operating range to prevent (when the movements are combined) the servos exceeding their safe travel range.

## Data reset

By activating this option the memory of the particular model being programmed is totally cleared and the settings return to the pre-set factory positions and values. This memory is then released for re-setting or for another model.

## Snap roll

To achieve a positive snap roll (also known as a flick roll) it is necessary to introduce control surface movements of aileron, elevator and rudder, the other factors determining the snap roll being the entry speed and attitude of the model. By programming the desired amounts of each control the snap roll can be selected at the touch of a button on the transmitter, the

directions, right or left and up and down, being available. When the snap roll button is depressed the aileron, elevator and rudder stick movements are inhibited, and normal control is only resumed on the release of the button.

## Auto rudder dual rate

When a model is flying slowly the rudder control is less effective, and during the landing phase, where the rudder is the primary directional control, it can be an advantage to have a higher rate of rudder movement. The auto rudder dual rate feature brings in the high rudder rate at a selected throttle position.

## Programmable mixing functions

In addition to the quoted mixing functions, the facility is also available to mix any of the nine or ten functions as seven or eight different mixings. The limits of these mixed functions are only limited by the requirements of the model and of your imagination.

For instance, instead of having the auto rudder dual rate, just described, you might prefer to have a rudder trim tab mixed, proportionally, with the throttle movement, to allow for the increased torque from the propeller as the engine speed increases. Spoilers and ailerons can be mixed to improve turning on sailplanes and unconventional designs, and flaps and air brakes combined to create more lift and drag for landings. Lowering an undercarriage may result in a fairly drastic pitch trim change, and mixing arrangements could be used to cope with this.

One of the difficulties in having such an extensive range of control function options with modern computer-controlled outfits is in

finding suitable words to explain the workings of the functions and how to program them. Here, from one of the manufacturer's brochures (admittedly translated from the Japanese) is one description of a mixing method:

'"Super" Mix. If 100% of mixing value is not enough, you can use a second mix and mix more, or less, as the case may be, into the mix. For example: We'll mix the throttle channel to itself and remove the throttle for certain aerobatic manoeuvres. If 100% is not enough, simply use another programmable mix (same channels, offset, mixing operator, etc) and take the throttle out further.'

And airline pilots think they have problems!

## Elevator to flap mixing

A common feature on aerobatic control-line ('U control') models was to interconnect the wing flaps with the elevator. This was a purely mechanical linkage, moving the flaps down as the elevator went up, and was operational at all times. With this coupling the radius of turn was increased considerably over the purely elevator-initiated turns. With the programmable mixing of elevator and flap on an R/C system there are the further advantages of being able to adjust the amounts of both functions, in both directions, and having it switchable.

## Landing systems – sailplanes

By the mixing of the elevator, flaps and spoilers (drag increasing) on the wings, the sailplane is set up for more consistent landing approaches. Modern sailplanes and gliders have low drag values and, without the application of flaps and spoilers, would tend to float on past the landing area.

## Landing attitude system – powered aircraft

Most of us have sat in an airliner on its final approach to land and watched the flaps extend and, on some jets, the spoilers appear vertically out of the wing to 'dump' the lift. With our models we can achieve similar results by pre-programming the flaps to extend, or depress, at certain throttle settings, and, if fitted, spoilers to extend at a safe (low) throttle position. Pitch trim changes caused by these applications, which may be nose-up or nose-down, can be countered by the automatic resetting of the elevator position as the flaps and spoilers are activated. The system can be switched in or out during flight.

## Undercarriage retract speed variation

With a full-size aeroplane the undercarriage never slams up or down at a tremendous speed – to do so would require enormous motivating power and would almost certainly damage the aircraft. With the speed variation function the speed of servo operation for the model undercarriage can be varied between 0.5 and 5.0 seconds, but you must ensure that the servo is suitable for this slow-speed movement. Obviously this facility is only suitable for mechanical retract operation, or a pneumatic system where a valve has a compatible servo operation.

## Servo test

The servo test function enables you to check whether the servos have developed any worn or 'dead' spots on their 'pots' (potentiometers). All linkages should be disconnected before the test is made to allow the servos to travel to their full movements. The servos

are programmed to cycle slowly through their range, and worn 'pot' tracks will usually be indicated by the servo output 'jittering'.

## Fail-safe/hold

This term, as previously mentioned, may be a misnomer, but it indicates that, on the failure of a 'clean' transmitter signal through interference, the servos will either take up pre-set positions or hold their last settings before the interference caused the fail-safe to operate. As soon as the signal is returned the equipment will function as before, and none of the programmed settings, trims, mixes, etc, will be lost. This system only operates on PCM transmissions and it cannot be totally disabled on some outfits.

In most instruction manuals the fail-safe is claimed to minimise the damage to your aeroplane during the loss of the signal to the receiver. If the controls are pre-set to go to the neutral position, or with a slight pitch stability setting and moderately low throttle, this could be true of an inherently stable model. However, fail-safe is a term that should more relate to the persons and buildings in the flying area rather than to the model. In other words the model should be fail-safe trimmed for the aeroplane to crash in the minimum distance, ie for the engine to cut entirely (the most potentially dangerous part of the model is a rotating propeller), and for full-up elevator plus full-right rudder and aileron. The model would thus spin or spiral down and cover the minimum distance across the ground – an important consideration if you are flying in front of the public.

Fortunately the equipment is, given correct installation and servicing, very reliable and is unlikely to move into the fail-safe

mode – also assuming that good frequency control is observed and that, for public functions, a frequency monitor is employed to check constantly for any outside interference.

## Model name input

This function is used to name and number each model in the transmitter memory, making it a simple and rapid action to change from one model to another, with all the function, trim, direction and quantity changes required. It is also possible to list the frequency used on the individual model, should a frequency change be necessary.

## Trim offset adjustment

During test flights it may be necessary to introduce trim adjustments on the transmitter trim levers to obtain the flying attitudes required of the model. Use of the trim offset allows you to reset electronically to these new neutrals and to return the trim levers to their centre positions.

## Trim rate adjustment

A selectable rate of either 50 or 100 per cent can be applied to the aileron, elevator and rudder functions. If 'one notch' on the transmitter trim lever is giving too much response, the rate should be reduced to the 50 per cent figure.

## Model selection

In addition to giving you the ten different model settings within the transmitter memory, this permits the copying of one model memory to another model.

## Modulation selection

This is used to select the type of PCM or PPM (Pulse Position Modulation, or FM) according to the receiver being used in the model.

## Data transfer

This feature is used to pass the memory of a model from one transmitter to another transmitter of the same type.

## Timer

Both an integrated timer and a count-down timer are featured. The integrated timer will display the accumulated time usage of each model stored in the transmitter memory, while the count-down feature is used as a stopwatch for timing individual flights, a bleeper sounding at 1-minute intervals, and more frequently as it moves from 30 seconds to zero.

## Keyboard lock

Inserting a three-digit code provides a safeguard against unwanted tampering with the transmitter settings. Unless the key-code is inserted there can be no access to the settings – so write the code down and store it in a safe place, because if you forget it the transmitter will have to be returned to the servicing agent to be unlocked.

## Special features – helicopter outfit

Many of the functions of the fixed-wing aeroplane transmitter are also available on the helicopter version. Indeed, the terms aileron, elevator, rudder and throttle may be used with the helicopter transmitter instructions, and although not aerodynamically correct definitions, they are well understood. To these functions is added a fifth 'primary' function for the helicopter – pitch (rotor) control.

The following features are common to the fixed-wing and helicopter sets: Model memories, modulation options, servo reversing, 'end point' adjustment (ATV), dual rates, exponential, combined linear and exponential rates, variable trace rates, sub-trim, fail-safe, low battery alarm, tuner, direct servo control, trainer system, model memory copy, data transfer and key-code lock.

Helicopter-only features include the following:

## Throttle hold

This feature maintains the throttle servo in a pre-determined position, a useful feature when practising autorotation landings.

## Throttle curves

By offering three separate throttle curves, each with five adjustable points per curve, it is possible to match the throttle curve and pitch curve to maximise the engine performance at a particular pitch setting. With the throttle curves established, the three-position switch will offer one normal and two stunt positions. The Normal position is used at the hover throttle curve, and Stunt 1 and 2 are used for aerobatic manoeuvres and forward flight. Throttle Trim and Hovering Throttle knob control are only operable in the Normal position. It is also possible to limit the high point in the latter setting. The Throttle Trim lever is also used to make adjustments to the engine idle speed and does not change the input values for the throttle curve points. For increasing or decreasing the engine output on the three middle points of the throttle curve (only in the Normal position) the Hovering Throttle knob is adjusted.

## Stunt trim

With the helicopter flying in a straight line at full throttle/pitch the model is electronically trimmed (elevator, rudder and aileron) for the Stunt 1 and 2 positions.

## Swash plate type adjuster

To ease the installation of swash plate linkages for helicopters that employ collective cyclic pitch mix (CCPM) there is a selection of swash type systems:

1 Single servo standard: the normal helicopter arrangement non CCPM.
2 Two servo: 180 degrees pitch and aileron channel connections.
3 Three servo: 120 degrees pitch, aileron and elevator connections.
4 Four servo: 90 degrees pitch, aileron, elevator and Aux 3 connections.

CCPM is a type of pitch mixing where the servos are connected directly to the swash plate and physically move the plate for all changes in pitch.

## Pitch curves

Adjustments of the pitch curve are similar to those for the throttle curves, and there are pitch curves available for the Normal, Stunt 1, Stunt 2 and Hold settings. The Hovering Pitch knob operates in a similar manner to the Hovering Throttle knob, shifting the middle portion of the curve upwards or downwards, in the Normal position only. To stay within the main rotor speed limitations of the manufacturer's specifications, the Pitch Trim knob is adjusted either side of a neutral point.

## Inverted flight switch

Although some helicopter pilots fly inverted by simply operating the specific controls in the opposite sense, most operators find it easier to have the Collective, Rudder and Elevator functions electronically reversed. This is activated by a switch on the tip of

*Transmitters are expensive, vulnerable products and deserve careful treatment. Purpose-made carrying cases are available for the transmitter and module.*

the transmitter. For inverted hovering manoeuvres the flight mode switch is left in the Normal position, while for inverted aerobatic manoeuvres a pitch curve should be programmed for inverted flight.

## Revolution mixing

This function adjusts the tail rotor pitch with the Throttle/Collective function variations and counteracts the torque from the main rotor blades. When correctly set, the helicopter should ascend and descend with no tendency to yaw in either direction. Because the main rotor torque reaction relates to different power settings, there are two revolution mixing programs, one for the Normal position and one for the Stunt 1 and 2 flight mode positions.

## Acceleration mixing

Acceleration and deceleration of the main rotor blades will also cause a torque reaction, compensated by varying the tail rotor pitch accordingly. Compensatory tail rotor settings will be at their maximum when the throttle movements are rapid, and less so when the engine speed variations are smooth and even.

## Free mixers

Up to five programmable mixes, of any pairs of channels (functions), are available, taking one channel as the master and mixing the other channel as the slave. The mixes can be left on permanently, or switched on and off in flight.

## Rotor direction

This allows the direction of rotor rotation, clockwise or counter-clockwise, to be programmed.

## Inverted pitch

This function is used to activate inverted flight functions and allows the inverted flight operation to use the normal flight functions by switching in the Inverted switch.

## Gyro sensitivity

Adjustment can be made to the gyro sensitivity by either two-position or linear switching, including exponential curve settings.

## Alternative expansion systems

In describing the transmitters so far we have dealt with complete units incapable of being modified; we have considered four-, six-, eight- and nine- or ten-function outfits as comprehensive items with the capabilities and limitations of the systems. There is, however, an alternative means of going from a basic outfit to a 'professional unit' capable of all the control functions that one would expect with a top-class system.

The advantages of these extendable outfits are fairly obvious; it is possible to start with a basic four-function, no frills system and add to it extra functions and facilities as required.

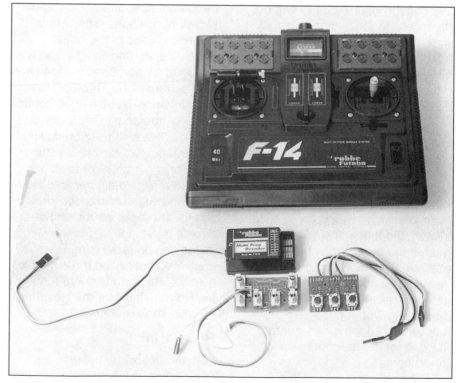

*A multi-options module system will allow you to add to the system with regard to the number of functions and facilities you require. The transmitter here is in the basic configuration, for car operation.*

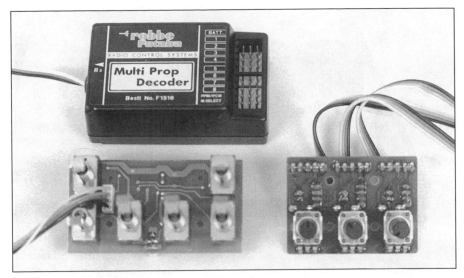

*Expandable systems are also available in the PCM computerised range, giving a high degree of selectability for additional functions and maximum flexibility in choosing the facilities for individual requirements. Modules are available in switched or proportional operation, and are installed in the top transmitter panels.*

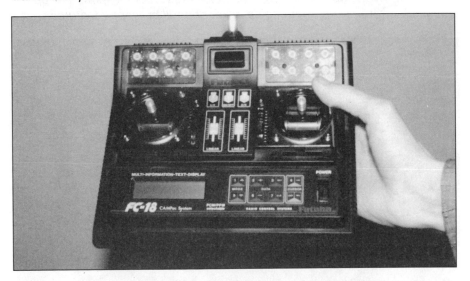

have servo reversing facilities on the four basic functions. From this basis the transmitter can be customised to increase the facility by adding a mini-option of switchable mixing, rate switches for two functions and multi-switching and multi-proportional modules to expand the uses to as many as 14 functions. The multi-modules only take one proportional channel of the receiver, but, through the micro-processor-controlled decoder, they allow up to eight switched or proportional functions to be operated from the transmitter – simultaneously, if this should be necessary.

With the computer-programmable outfits the module options are much greater and include mixer switches, channel switches, mixer trimmers, stick switches (a miniature toggle switch fitted to the main control stick), dual rate modules, instructor/student trainer systems, data storage module and multi-proportional and switch banks. With the top-of-the-range PCM transmitters all the functions mentioned in the non-expandable transmitters are available, and considerably more functions from the eight channels.

Glider, helicopter and fixed-wing aircraft are all catered for with the specialist mixings, helicopter setting curves, etc, plus tachometer, timing systems, transmitter and receiver voltage checking facilities, PCM/FM transmissions, trainer mode, fail-safe, data transfer and Quattro rate function. The latter AFR (adjustable function rate) allows the servo rate for all channels and mixed functions to be set for up to four different flight parameters. With a glider it would be possible to set these rates for the best launch, fast flight, duration and

Thus you might start with an FM non-computerised or PCM computerised basic package and extend it by adding modules to the transmitter to increase the operating potential. Having the add-on modules plus, on the receiver side, an additional decoder, gives the flexibility of increasing the specification and options when you decide you are ready; but you will have to make the initial decision of whether to

set out on a standard FM system, a computerised FM system or a fully programmable PCM system with large graphics display screen and the facility for virtually unlimited model memory storage. With exchangeable RF modules the transmitters can be used for all frequency bands, making them suitable for aircraft, cars or boats in any country.

For the non-computerised FM system the standard basic will

landing characteristics.

Helicopter and fixed-wing modellers will obtain the most use from the extra facilities available with the extendable systems, but scale boating enthusiasts will find the multi-switching and multi-proportional modules of interest. Operation of anchors, fire monitors, cranes, searchlights and small boat deployment for Merchant Navy vessels, and various weaponry, including guided missiles, for military ships, can be actuated through these optional modules.

A further method on the expansion theme is to have a standard six-function FM and, as more features are required, to fit an LCD panel to the transmitter. This, together with the optional switches and mixers, allows the outfit to be upgraded to a mid-range programmable system with a three-model memory. Fitting the optional modules to the expandable systems requires no electronic or electrical knowledge; it is a simple matter of plugging on to the transmitter printed circuit board and fitting the switch, knob or slider to the console.

Working out the economics or the expandable and non-expandable systems is not easy, as forecasting future requirements is little better than inspired guesswork. You may find that today's interest in racing electric cars leads you on to the more three-dimensional activity of flying fixed-wing model aeroplanes, and this, in turn, to the challenging aspects of helicopter flying. Certainly in the initial stages it is difficult to comprehend the full potential of the available radio systems, and probably impossible to know the final direction of your modelling interests. For this reason it would seem prudent to purchase in the first instance a 'standard' FM

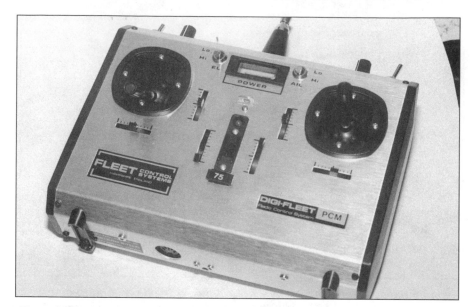

*Fleet Control Systems' PCM system has seven channels and all the mixing functions, servo and throw adjustment, plus fail-safe. They also produce a multi-mode version for fixed-wing, glider, twin-engine and helicopter, which has, in addition, 'end point' adjustment, exponential dual rates, full 'crow' mixing, twin-engine mixer and full helicopter features.*

outfit, non-programmable and with four or six functions.

By the time you have reached the useful limits of this outfit, whether it is on cars, boats or aircraft, you will have a much better idea of the particular modelling discipline you want to follow, and it should be a little easier to make your next selection. Whether this will be a fully

integrated system or the expandable type may depend on the capital available at the time of purchase, but do take the trouble to calculate the comparative costs of the two methods of reaching the same final specification. It may pay you to borrow the money, or buy by hire purchase, and obtain the full specification system from the beginning.

To complicate the decision-making even further you may be confronted with a choice of transmitter styles. The 'oblong box', whether it has rounded corners or top, remains the most popular format, but some modellers prefer the 'European' style of transmitter. This features a sloped-top console (making it more suitable for the expandable systems) containing the auxiliary controls. Although this style of transmitter can be hand-held, the top-heavy balance makes it more suited to strap or tray operation.

## Experiment

There is little point in purchasing a transmitter capable of giving you a vast range of mixing, coupling, variable rates and similar facilities if these controls are left untouched. It can be great fun trying out these functions, and with a fixed-wing aircraft it will give you options that were denied to the full-size aircraft test pilots. Providing that you can switch the combinations in or out during flight, and that you have plenty of height to recover if the control turns out to be unworkable, you have nothing to lose.

You may find that a previously difficult model to fly is transformed by, for example, introducing differential movement on the ailerons, or coupling aileron and rudder control. Getting past the initial test flights may be the biggest problem, but once this goal has been achieved you can go on to fine-tune the model by using all the electronic devices at your command. With so many alternatives of mixes and programming I doubt whether a 'perfectly' trimmed model will ever be achieved, but it is interesting and exciting to continually extend the process of improvement.

We should also remember that experiments and adjustments are not confined to the electronics. Transmitters can have physical adjustments made to suit your style of operation. Control sticks can be shortened or lengthened and, in some cases, offset. Spring tensions on the sticks are also adjustable for soft or hard movement, and rubber grip pads on the rear of the transmitter case are an option on some outfits. Try the transmitter for feel and also see whether you are more comfortable with a free hand-hold, or with a neck strap, or a transmitter tray.

## Safety

All electronic and mechanical equipment needs checking and servicing periodically, and radio control equipment is no exception. Every year or two, depending on the amount of use the equipment has had, it should be returned to the servicing agent for checking. This is money well spent, as it could result in a fault being spotted before it has caused a crash. The servicing agent will have test equipment that can trace faults that we cannot hope to recognise by a simple visual inspection.

Radio equipment should also be returned for checking if it has been involved in a serious crash. Again, the equipment may appear to be undamaged and may seem to be working normally, but it is prudent to have it tested before it is used again. Never try to tell the servicing agent anything less than the full story regarding the history of the equipment. If the crash was a result of pilot error, be man enough to admit it; pretending that it was caused by an electronic failure is not going to help trace the faults – or reduce the bill. It is more likely to have the opposite result.

I suggested earlier that when the equipment is first installed in a model, range checks should be carried out, both with the engine not running and running. This can be done with the transmitter aerial collapsed, but should be

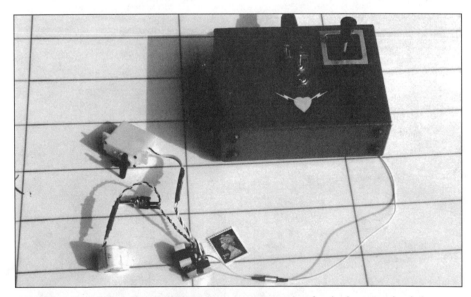

*Micro radio equipment is becoming more popular for indoor and mini-model flying. This World Electronics outfit has a postage-stamp-size receiver, 3.6 volt 50mAh battery and single Union servo; the total airborne weight is a couple of ounces.*

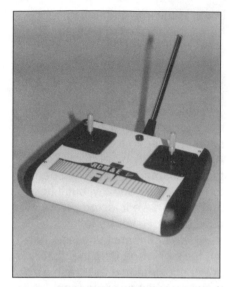

*At one time DIY radio equipment was quite popular, but now very few modellers take the trouble to build their own radios, either from scratch or from kits. The exception is with FM receivers, where the cost of the kits makes them a reasonable proposition.*

undertaken when no other transmitters are being operated and at an area clear of buildings, power lines, etc, for example your modelling site on a non-operating day. Information logged should include range distances before control is no longer reliable, and the conditions of the tests –

where, when, and the temperature.

From time to time further range tests should be made with the equipment, with the previous information used as a base. If, under relatively similar conditions, there is a major change in working ranges, you should suspect a problem with the equipment.

Check the installation, the batteries for full charging, the transmitter aerial for cleanliness and the receiver aerial for suitable location, then carry out further range checks. If the range is still down, return the equipment to the servicing agent for testing.

Always treat your radio equipment with respect. Never strain servo or battery leads by excessive pulling on them, even though it is difficult to remove some servo plugs from the receiver connecting block without some pulling on the leads; it may be safer to ease the plugs from the receiver using medical tweezers. When the linkage or hinging does not allow the servo to move through its full arc, including trim movements, it will protest by making a 'buzzing' noise. If you hear this distressing sound find the cause of the movement limitation and take action to clear the obstruction, or, if this is not possible, reduce the effective movement of the servo by electronic means or by moving the take-off position on the output closer to the centre.

*A look into the future? This is the prototype design for a twin-frequency transmitter with a fail-safe device that automatically cuts to the reserve frequency if the primary frequency is subjected to interference.*

# Chapter 3

# Ancillaries

Many products are marketed for operation in conjunction with radio control outfits to expand the uses of the equipment or to make the operation of the models easier.

## Revolution counter

One function sometimes fitted to transmitters, and not listed in the previous chapter, is a revolution counter. Where this is incorporated in the transmitter the 'eye' is located on the side, the programme is set for a two- or three-bladed propeller and the rpm (revolutions per minute) is then given on the LDC. This is particularly useful for scale multi-engined models where comparative speeds and reliability of engine operation are vitally important. Other transmitters may also include facilities for twin-engined helicopters, but if you require a function to equalise the speed of engines in a multi-engined fixed-wing model you will usually have to purchase a separate unit.

## Fail-safe

As we have seen in the previous chapter, fail-safes are normally only fitted to PCM outfits, and if you want to have a fail-safe installed in a model with an FM (PPM) radio, it will have to be fitted as a separate item. Fail-safes are available in single-function (to cut the engine only) and four-function types, and it is normally possible to adjust the delay time between when the

signal is lost and the time the fail-safe is activated. Too short a delay period will activate the fail-safe with even the shortest period of interference, while too long a delay might make it impossible to save the model when the signal has actually returned.

## Frequency crystals

Economy outfits have plug-in frequency crystals, and these are interchangeable within that waveband only; in other words you cannot fit 40MHz crystals in a 35MHz transmitter and receiver and expect it to work. The alternative crystals must be for the correct frequency band and for the correct signal modulation

(FM/PPM, PCM or AM). Always purchase the manufacturer's recommended crystals, as other makes may not work in different systems. The more advanced radio control outfits have removable modules for the transmitters containing the crystal and the RF (radiated frequency) section. This has the advantage that a 35MHz transmitter can, by changing the module, be made to operate on 40MHz or 72MHz, a real bonus for modellers operating their models in different countries. The receivers, however, are not convertible, and it is necessary to purchase a receiver to match the alternative frequency band (eg 40 or 72MHz) selected for the transmitter.

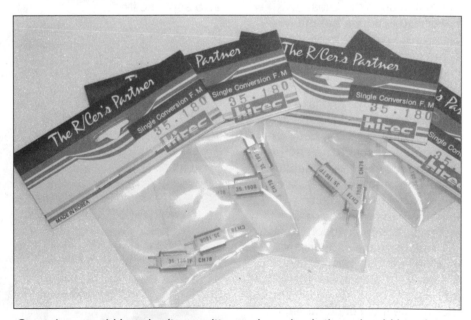

*Crystals are sold in pairs (transmitter and receiver); they should be of the correct make, correct type (single or double conversion for receiver) and correct transmission type (FM or PCM).*

## Frequency monitor

Not an item that is individually purchased very often, but one that can save many a crash, a frequency monitor can be set to scan the transmitter frequencies in operation at any R/C model site and display those being used. By the same token it will also indicate any spurious signals being picked up by the monitor. Although not foolproof – for aeroplanes it would ideally be positioned in the air where the planes are flying – it is a sound investment by any club or group. If it does nothing else, it will show if a transmitter is operating on a frequency not indicated on the transmitter frequency pennant. This error is, regrettably, all too frequent. A modeller changes crystals to another 'spot' frequency and forgets to change the pennant – and, next time out, has forgotten that he has changed!

## Other add-on functions

For modellers with outfits that do not match up to the latest specifications there are many electronic 'gadgets' to provide some of the missing functions. For instance, there is a 'Servo-Slow' unit that is installed between the receiver and servo and is adjustable to slow down the total movement of the servo between 0.5 and 7.5 seconds. It performs the same function as the feature on the top-of-the-range PCM outfit, and is suitable for retracting undercarriage systems or, for instance, bomb-bay doors.

Undercarriage sequencing modules are available, which, from one receiver output, can program for operation and speed the servos moving the main undercarriage wheels and legs and the undercarriage doors. They are available in two forms, one where

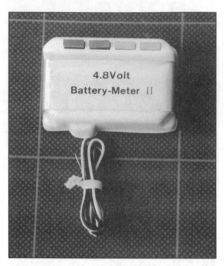

*Battery state checking, for the receiver pack, can be done from an on-board meter, installed so that indicator lights are visible from the outside.*

the doors retract between the wheels coming down and going up again.

Electronic differential controls (to give more upgoing than downgoing aileron) are standard on computer outfits, but units are also available as separate items. The same applies to mixers – if your outfit does not feature a mixer control, it can be also purchased as a separate item.

## Testing and checking

Nicad battery voltage checkers, for the receiver packs, can be of the on-board type, where it is permanently fitted to the model and usually has the LEDs exposed for quick reference. Alternatively they can be of the plug-in type, which is connected to check the battery voltage (with the system operating under load), then removed.

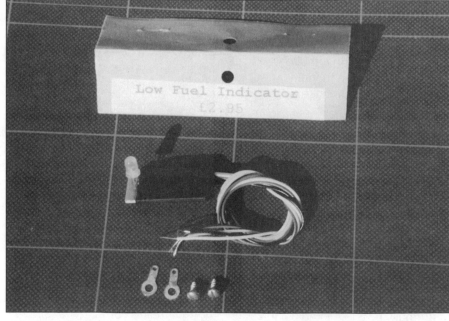

*An on-board low fuel state indicator is useful for helicopter flyers.*

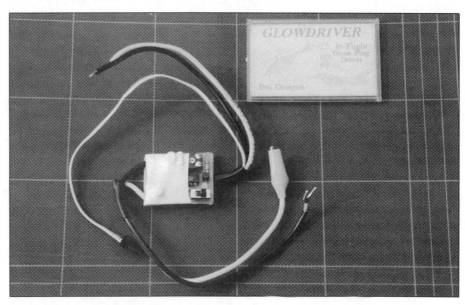

*In-flight glow plug drivers will help prevent a 'glo' engine from cutting at low idle speeds.*

Very few radio control manufacturers provide surface-mounting charging sockets with their equipment, and it is normally a matter of delving into the innards of the model to retrieve the socket – or plug – to connect it to the charger. Surface-mounting charging sockets are available as an accessory and they would also allow, for example, the nicad checker to be plugged in for a quick voltage check.

For modellers paranoid about running out of fuel during a flight there is a neat little unit that will light an LED when the fuel level is running low.

'Glo' engines are most likely to unexpectedly stop at low throttle settings. This is because the glow of the plug is less intense at lower speeds and raw fuel may extinguish it and cause the engine to cease running. One option to reduce the risk of this happening is to energise the plug at the lower throttle settings, and although this can be done by fitting a micro-switch to operate it from the throttle servo (cutting in a 1.2 volt nicad battery) there is now a device that can be fitted between the receiver and servo and which can be adjusted for the point of the battery being switched.

Servo testers and in-line servo-centring products will do for the economy outfit what is already incorporated in the computer sets, and one item not to be found – as yet – on any R/C system is the battery backer. Although nicad cells rarely fail, even this small risk is unacceptable for large-scale models, in relation to both safety and expense.

## Ancillaries for larger models

There are no specific R/C systems designed for large models, as there are for helicopters for instance, but perhaps this will change in the future. The manufacturers argue that all the modeller wishing to fly large models has to do, is to buy an outfit with a fail-safe, then purchase large, powerful servos and large airborne battery packs.

There is, though, rather more than that to the fitting of R/C equipment to really large models.

With extra-long servo leads additional precautions have to be taken, and as many systems and components should be duplicated as possible. The battery backer, where two batteries are fitted for the one receiver pack, the secondary battery being automatically activated in the event of the primary battery failing, solves one problem (an LED will show if the second battery is being used). A separate battery supply, probably 6 volt, may be used to power the servos, giving another safety factor.

When radio equipment is being installed in large models with additional battery supplies and more than one servo from one output, etc, it is sensible to use a purpose-designed junction board. These are available and will eliminate to a large degree the 'rat's nest' of wires. Extension leads, Y leads and switch harnesses are readily available for all manufacturers' outfits, and there are companies prepared to make up wiring looms to order. If you are less than handy with a soldering iron, this type of service is highly recommended.

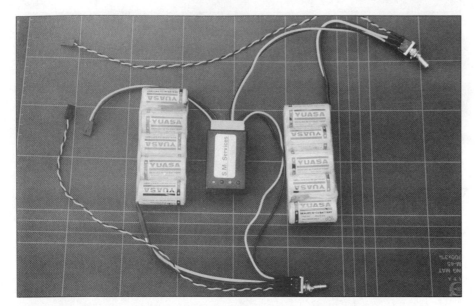

*Dual battery systems should have separate charging sockets for the batteries, and can have LEDs to indicate charge state or, as in Francis Plessier's circuit, shown here, a warning buzzer when the back-up battery has come into operation – which it will do automatically when the main battery voltage drops below a safe level. The second diagram shows a simple alternative battery back-up system.*

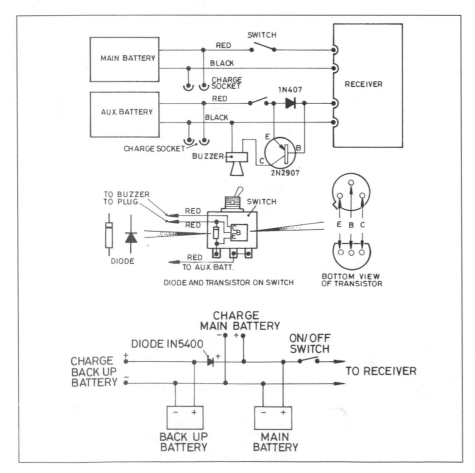

On/off switches can easily be contaminated if fitted to a model externally and mechanics for remotely operating them should be used wherever possible – especially where the switch is subjected to dirt and water.

## Ancillaries for electric power

At the opposite end of the R/C model spectrum, there are more products being introduced for miniaturisation, particularly with regard to receivers, servos and batteries. The reduction in size and weight of the components installed in the model is benefiting the electric-powered boat, car and aircraft modeller, and the potential size of the models is reducing all the time. Electric-powered helicopters are now commonplace, thanks to the improvements in batteries and reduced R/C equipment sizes; a few years ago they were an experimenter's ultimate challenge.

It is not only the receivers, batteries and servos that have been miniaturised; just as important for the electric power enthusiast are the physically small speed controllers now commercially available. These used to be large units with heavy heat sink to dissipate the heat build-up, but now it is possible to purchase a combined electronic speed controller, with forward, brake and reverse facilities, thermal overload protection and BEC (battery eliminator circuitry) with a total weight of around 70 g.

The latter unit, the BEC, is also available as a separate item and allows the use of one battery to power the electric motor and the lower voltage receiver. When the voltage drops to a pre-determined figure, the BEC switches off the

*Separate aileron servos in each wing panel require Y leads. These can have signal boosters and a choke to prevent the signal being returned down the leads, where these are long.*

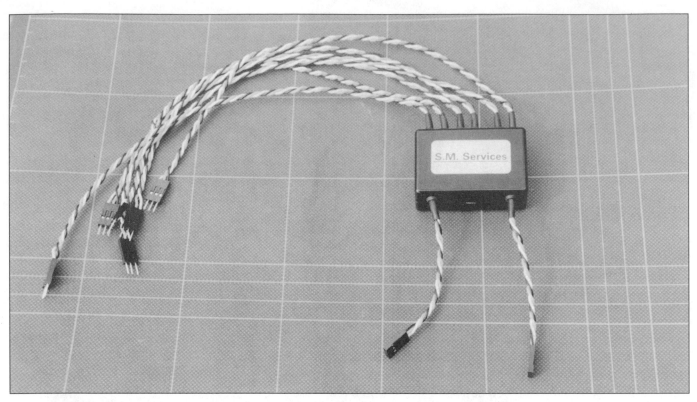

*A junction board is ideal for large models where servo lead extensions are needed; chokes are fitted between the connectors, and additional systems such as a battery-backer and fail-safe are required. The servo lead splitter takes the output from two servo outputs and divides them into two (twin-engine throttles) and four (ailerons on all wings of a biplane) servo connectors.*

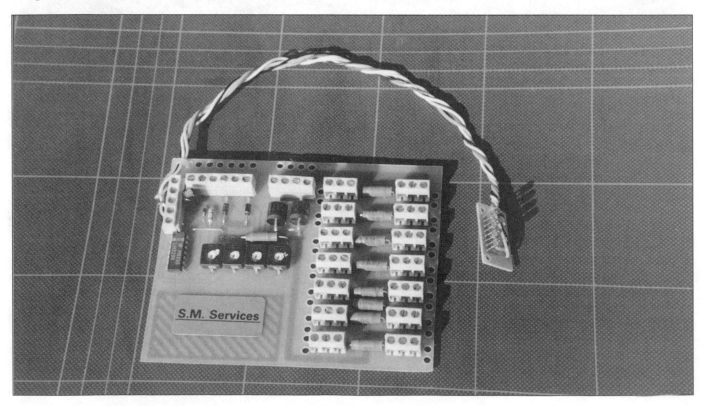

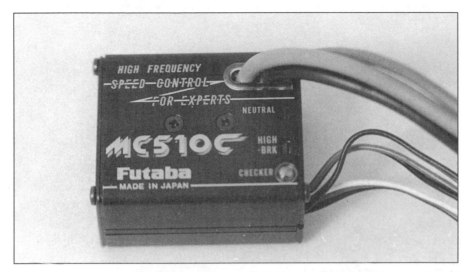

Electronic speed controllers combine overload protection, BEC (battery eliminator circuitry) and, where required, reversing and braking. Sizes of the controllers have reduced dramatically.

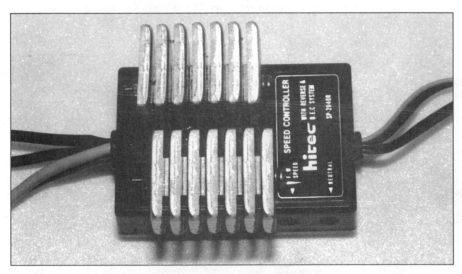

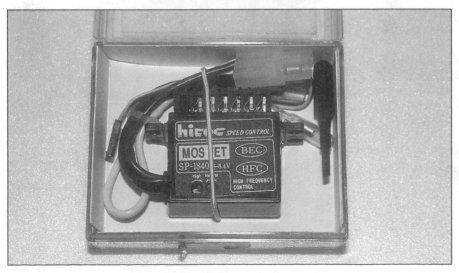

motor and the receiver is then given priority for the remaining life of the battery – adequate to return the model safely.

Simple electric switches are available for straight 'on' and 'off' functions, although these may be obtained with a 'soft start' to prevent a sudden surge of electric motor power. For electric flight they can also be supplied with a brake at the 'off' position to allow a folding propeller to retain its folded location. Quick chargers are intended for the motor power nicad battery packs and should not normally be used for the receiver nicads, unless a common pack and BEC is being used. Extremely complex switching arrangements can be designed for surface vehicles, or scale aircraft models, either initiated by the servo output or as separate functions actuated by a transmitter control.

With environmental considerations an important part of everyone's life, the importance of electric power cannot be overstressed. The quiet operation, lack of smell and cleanliness offer many advantages over IC (internal combustion) engine power, and allow models to be safely operated from public areas that would otherwise be banned to modellers. However, the lack of noise and smell may not be to every modeller's taste, and there are many – and I have to include myself – that enjoy 'tinkering' with glow, diesel and spark ignition engines; what may be fumes to some are 'perfumes' to another group! With regard to noise, someone compared the racing of electric-powered pylon racers to a Grand Prix with electric milk floats! Not quite fair, but an understandable comment.

For sure, we all have to live together in our crowded world and whatever our hobby, or whatever form the hobby takes, we must give due consideration to our neighbours. If we take our 'toys' (and how some modellers hate their models to be referred to in such terms – be warned!) on holiday, it would certainly be sensible to only take battery-powered models where there is no noise or mess to cause annoyance. Fortunately the equipment manufacturers have thought about this possibility and have designed 'Holiday Chargers', which operate off 12 volts, for example a car battery.

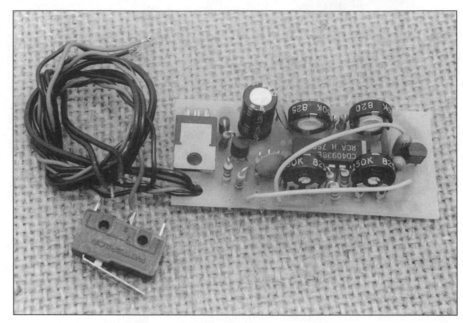

*An electronic device to make more noise! This unit is designed to simulate machine-gun fire.*

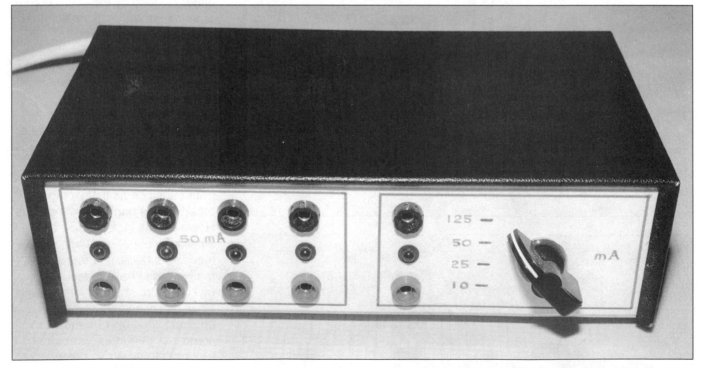

*Above and opposite: Standard rate chargers, mains or battery operated, battery cyclers, analysers, field fast chargers and battery-operated 'Holiday' chargers are all available to keep your nicad packs fully charged and in good health.*

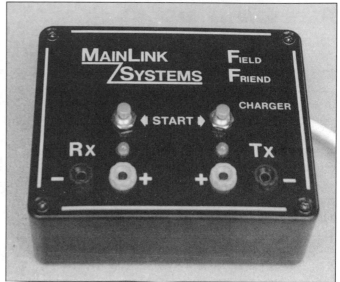

## Sound generators

For boats and specialist surface vehicles (fire engines, police cars, etc) it is possible to purchase 'sound generators', which are directly switched via the transmitter. If there is no problem in producing a wailing siren, bells and similar noises, it is reasonable to assume that the simulation of jet engines, machine-gun fire and dropping bombs would be feasible. This could add considerably to the 'believability' of electric-powered model aeroplanes.

## Air-to-ground transmissions

Going up-market, there are now on-board measurement systems that will tell, for instance, the speed of the model, the climb rate, height, battery voltage, engine speed and presumably, if you require it, the engine cylinder temperature. There are not many modelling activities where these could be put to good use, they are likely to be banned from competitions and they may well be illegal to operate; transmitting from an airborne model to the ground is forbidden in certain countries. This is primarily, one presumes, to prevent unlawful video camera surveillance of 'sensitive' areas, and, as so often happens, one regulation precludes the use of quite innocent activities.

However, the operation of 'still' cameras, fitted to aircraft models of weights lower than the Aviation Authorities' exemption levels, may be used because in these cases the operating signal is only being transmitted from the ground to the air.

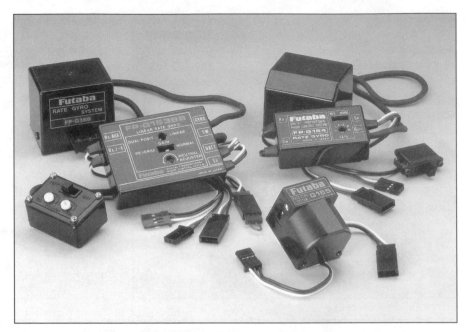

*Gyro systems are mostly used for helicopter flying, although they have a potential in fixed-wing aeroplanes and have been used, experimentally, in cars to keep a straight course at the start of a race.*

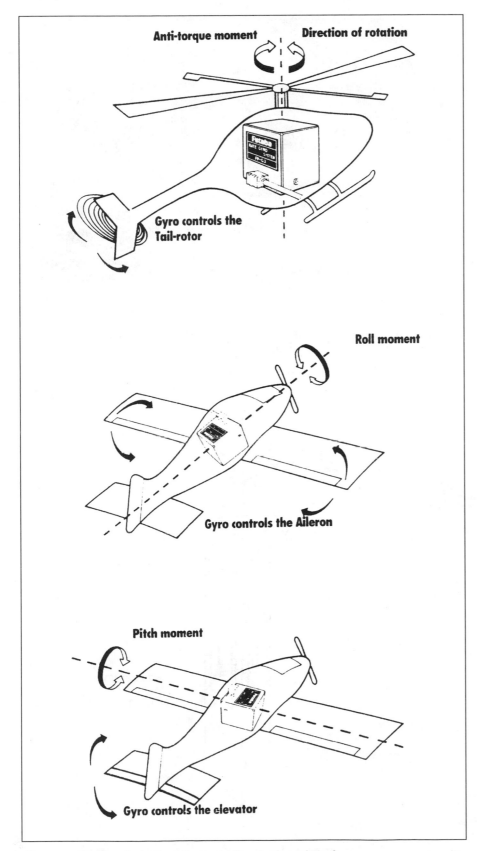

*Gyro application in helicopters and fixed-wing aircraft.*

## Gyros

The principles of gyro operation have been known for centuries, and we have probably played with gyro toys as children. If nothing else, we will have seen the action and reaction when a hand-held bicycle wheel is spun then attempted to be turned. We may not have been taught the terms 'precision', 'flywheel' and 'gyro effect', but we could follow the cause and effect in a practical way. It may not have stopped us from falling off our bicycle, but at least we had a better understanding of why we had fallen.

Gyros for models only came to prominence with the 'second generation' of helicopter models. As more advanced, higher-performance models came on to the market it became more difficult for the operator to control the yaw of the helicopter. With rapid changes of main rotor pitch and speed of the aircraft it was often a case of 'chase the tail', as the pilot could not feed in the tail rotor pitch changes sufficiently quickly to keep the helicopter from yawing.

Whether or not we like to admit it, electronics, computers and gyros are, in nearly all cases, quicker in action than our brains and hands. A miniature gyro fitted in a model helicopter will react virtually instantly to a change of direction (yaw) and will, if connected to the servo operating the tail rotor pitch, take the necessary corrective action. Unless overridden by the pilot the gyro, if correctly set up, will keep the helicopter facing in the same direction.

Our model gyro systems are quite small; they have a gyro wheel similar to the flywheel gyro toys except that they are spun by an electric motor and kept rotating at a constant speed. They have sensitivity control so that the degree of reaction can be adjusted; too much 'gain' and the model will oscillate (swing) to either side of a neutral position, too little sensitivity and the model will not return to the desired direction.

A gyro fitted to a helicopter assists in controlling the tail movements and it will dampen out the unwanted yaw movements, but it is a case of action and reaction; it will not totally prevent directional changes, and should be looked upon as an aid to smoother and neater flying. Consisting of the rotating flywheel gyro device, including drive motor, and the electronics package, it is fitted between the receiver and tail rotor servo. The gain, or sensitivity, of the gyro system is normally continuously variable from a separate transmitter control, although some are switchable (manually or electronically) from high to low rate and vice versa.

Gyro packages may consist of a single unit, housing the gyro, electronics and control, or as separate units; a separate battery supply is required for some gyros, while others operate from a receiver/servo battery pack of suitable capacity.

Gyros have not been extensively used in fixed-wing models, and their use is banned in FAI (Fédération Aeronautique International) scale competitions where they would be of most help to the pilot. The same applies to aerobatic contests, although the advantages for these models would be less – they do not keep in straight lines for very long periods.

The commercial world of scale model aircraft is one area where the gyro really comes into its own. Here it is necessary to emulate full-size aircraft; they must appear to be less influenced by air turbulence and have an apparently smoother flight pattern. Apparently,

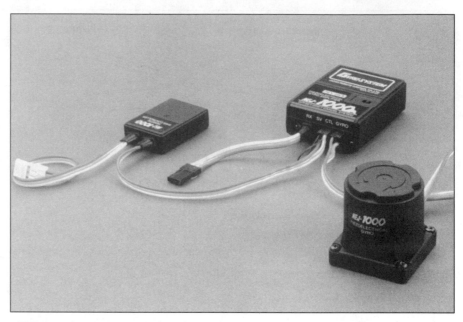

*JR have developed a solid state gyro with no motor or flywheel – or any moving parts that might wear out.*

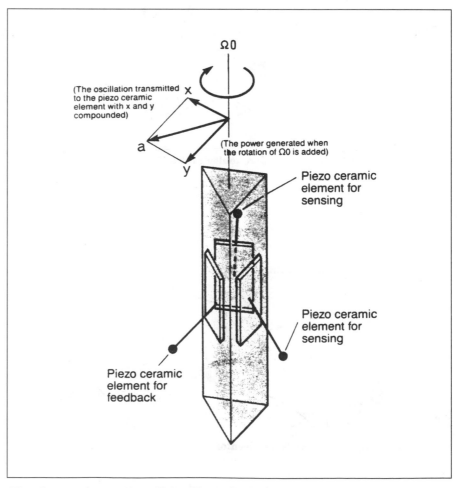

*The theory of operation of the Piezo Oscillating Gyro.*

because if you are sitting in a light aircraft on a windy day you will be buffeted about to quite a degree, while from the ground it looks to be quite a smooth flight. By fitting gyros in a scale model emulating a full-size aeroplane, many of the small disturbances can be 'ironed out', and from the ground, or through the camera lens, the model seems to be flying much more smoothly than would be possible without the use of gyros. The alternative to using individual gyros would be to fit a model autopilot, but more of that later.

One of the most exciting developments in the world of gyros recently is the solid state gyro system, representing a tremendous technological

breakthrough. Unlike standard electro-mechanical gyroscopes that use a motor and flywheel sensor, the piezoelectric gyro system is totally free of moving parts that might wear out, giving it a nearly unlimited service life while offering a tenfold increase in performance over current gyroscopes. The heart of the piezoelectric gyroscope is a small vibrating prism that detects the slightest change in angular velocity using the Coriolis effect.

### Vibration protection

The sensor unit is protected from vibration by a newly developed vibration isolation system. This is designed to prevent the ability of

the gyroscope to detect angular velocities as small as that of the earth's rotation and as large as 720 degrees per second from being impaired by the vibrations of the model in which it is installed. This system ensures the same high level of performance regardless of the installation and mounting method.

### Control of angular velocity

The purpose of a gyroscope is to damp out unwanted disturbances. With a conventional gyroscope the better this is achieved, the less control authority remains with the pilot. In extreme circumstances

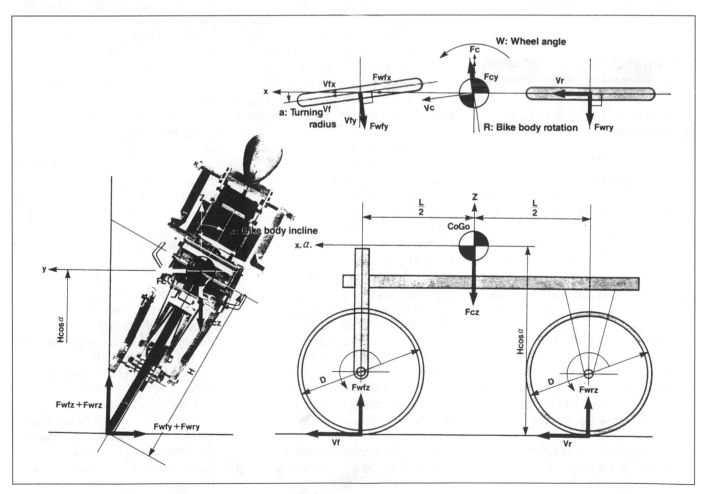

*Design parameters for the JR solid state 'gyro-bike'.*

there would be a complete loss of command, as all model movements would be prevented by the gyroscope! The NEJ-1000 senses the control commands and produces an angular velocity commensurate with the stick input; the model follows the pilot's commands in a smooth and precise manner.

## Drift cancellation

Temperature drift, which has been up to now the major and often fatal flaw in the design of high-performance vibrating gyroscopes, has been eliminated. Technical innovation has enabled the production of the first high-performance piezoelectric vibrating gyro system ahead even of the manufacturers of industrial gyroscopes.

## Remote gain controller

The preset high- and low-gain selection may be made remotely from the transmitter.

### Specification

Input voltage: 4.8 volts
Current consumption: 80MA
Dynamic range: 0 to 720 degrees per second
Dimensions:

|  | Length x width x height (mm) | Weight (g) |
|---|---|---|
| Sensor | 33 x 33 x 34 | 43 |
| Amplifier | 38 x 53 x 16 | 33 |
| Remote gain controller | 24 x 35 x 10 | 12 |

To demonstrate the amazing abilities of the new solid state gyro, the manufacturers, JR Propo (Japan Remote Control Co Ltd) were looking for a novel and 'fun' way to illustrate the practical operation of the product. Here is their description of this project:

To fully demonstrate that performance it was necessary to abandon current ideas and redesign the control circuits and system. Many difficult problems were solved and on the day of the evaluation test of the new gyro system, somebody asked, quite innocently, if the performance of this system couldn't be used elsewhere.

'It can ride a bike!' One staff member produced a report with pages full of calculations. That report was an analysis of a bicycle's mechanism and its operation by a human, with a mathematical equation that was used to develop the control theory. The basic mechanism works like this. The angular roll velocity (at which the bicycle is toppling over) is detected by the oscillating gyro, and it is kept upright by moving the centre of gravity with the centrifugal force created by the running speed and handlebar angle. By positively imposing an angular roll velocity, the bicycle can be turned on the move. The report was evaluated as being 'very possible', and so began the bicycle project.

The aim was to run unsupported on two wheels, as slowly as possible, with the direction controlled by radio control. Of course it had to be totally electronically controlled with no flywheel or other mechanical stabilising aid whatsoever. It wasn't long before the sound of crashing bicycles could be heard late into the night from the test lab and along the corridors.

One month had passed since the trials had begun, but the bike was still not running properly, proving that although it was possible in theory, it was very difficult in practice.

The time spent on the project and the confidence and spirit that had helped the engineers along thus far were slowly beginning to fade. Despite this, there was still a belief in the tremendous ability of man.

Most people who are normally agile can ride a bicycle. Humans also have the ability to move unconsciously and extremely accurately by inferring a given situation and moving sensors that cannot be matched by even the best high-tech electronics or mechanics. We realised that we were trying to do the same thing. We were trying to teach this piece of metal to balance on two wheels. Even if we couldn't match human ability, there was no problem with the ability of the 'oscillating gyro'. All we had to do was to put that into the computer that was controlling the handlebars.

'OK, so if the bike leans we turn the handlebars in the direction of the lean.'

'When it turns we turn the bike in the other direction.'

'Once it begins to turn, keep the handlebars in that direction so that there is no further lean.'

This exchange with the computer kept going and the bike kept falling over.

The 'crash course' continued for three months. One day the swishing sound of a bicycle moving was heard in the hallway. Normally this would soon be followed by a crashing noise loud enough to make one wince, but no such noise was heard. The swishing sound continued! It was running! All the researchers rushed out into the corridor. In the midst of that throng of people one member of staff knelt down, pointing to the microcomputer chip of the, by now, stopped bicycle, looked up and said 'He's finally done it!'

For those of you of a technical nature, who would like to know a little more about the Piezo Oscillating Gyro, here are a few more pointers from the manufacturers themselves.

The development of the equilateral triangular prismatic oscillator means that the left and right piezo ceramic elements can be positioned in the direction of the compound oscillating mode. This has made it possible to use one piezo ceramic element for both oscillating and sensing, allowing simpler construction and circuitry.

As a result, it is now possible to develop an extremely small angular velocity sensor that can be mass produced.

A new method that senses by subtracting the left and right outputs has been used. When there is no rotation (when moving directly ahead) any random oscillation from above or below or from shakes to front or back is also subtracted from left to right, effectively cancelling any noise and having no effect on angular detection. Furthermore, when there is rotation, by subtracting the detected left and right value, $(A + a) - (A - a) = 2a$, it gives a high sensor output. This method

produces a very high S/N ratio.

By placing the piezo ceramic element in the direction of the compound oscillation mode, it is possible to detect the change of oscillation through rotation at an angle close to the right angle, ensuring a great increase in the efficiency of piezo conversion.

Because, in principle, this method allows the resonance frequencies to be matched in three directions simultaneously, it can detect the smallest of angular accelerations and thereby achieve excellent linearity.

Elinvar elastically invariable metal has been used in the equilateral triangular prismatic oscillator, ensuring excellent temperature characteristics when combined with the piezo ceramic element.

Zero hysteresis has been achieved through high piezo conversion efficiency and unified three-direction resonance frequency. Precision is significantly better than other oscillating gyros.

## Autopilot control

Airliners have autopilots that allow take-offs and landings to be accomplished in 'blind' conditions, such as thick fog. They can also carry out these functions more accurately and consistently than the human pilot. In many respects the latter is only there in case something goes wrong, but because that could happen, he must also practice his manual take-off and landing procedures; thus the autopilot system often gives way to manual operation. Even so, the trainee pilot and the experienced pilot moving on to a new type of aircraft will carry out most of their 'practical' flying training in a simulator, another piece of electronic wizardry.

Model autopilots have nowhere near reached these standards of sophistication; all they will do is to regain a straight and level position when the model aeroplane has been disturbed from that attitude. For example, if the model has been placed, by outside forces or otherwise, into a diving turn to the left, on centralisation of the control sticks on the transmitter the model will regain its former straight and level flight. Not only that, but it will do so with a minimum of corrections and more rapidly than, probably, any model pilot could achieve.

Put a model fitted with the BTA autopilot into a vertical climb, let go of the control sticks and watch the autopilot take over. Depending on the precise attitude of the model, it will either 'push over' to a level keel, or 'pull over' and half roll out to level flight. It is quite uncanny to watch – you would credit it with more senses than it actually possesses. It will not regain a specific heading (direction), nor will it maintain a constant height, although it does, to some degree, regain some of

*The author fitted helicopter-style gyros to his Pronto-G trainer to evaluate their potential as a training aid. Although of some assistance, they did not provide the full advantages of the commercially available BTA autopilot, and HAL 2000 levelling system.*

the height lost in the manoeuvre made before the autopilot correction commenced.

This model autopilot was developed from a system used for military purposes. Obviously there is much to be gained if it is possible to fly unmanned aircraft over enemy areas for the purposes of camera surveillance, or perhaps to trigger off the anti-aircraft ground-to-air missiles. Where these missiles are automatically launched on picking up a sound or heat signal from an unidentified aircraft, it would be inexpensive in both money and life if they could be 'fooled' into firing at a radio-controlled 'drone' aircraft. Fitting an autopilot would allow the drones to be flown out of visual range of the operator and without the need for radar.

For camera surveillance, and for a radar control aircraft, it is still necessary to have some stabilising control in the pilotless aircraft, and the autopilot system will do this. The military versions are a little more complex than our types, and will maintain a constant height, while others will also maintain a heading.

Again, for the technically minded, here are some details of the BTA autopilot.

## BTA autopilot

The main function of the autopilot is to return the model automatically to a pre-programmed flight attitude (normally straight and level) when the transmitter control sticks are released. This is irrespective of the attitude of the model at the time, and the autopilot will even recover a model, given sufficient height, from an inverted dive.

Operating via aileron and elevator controls (the rudder and engine throttle are unaffected), the unit is plugged in between the

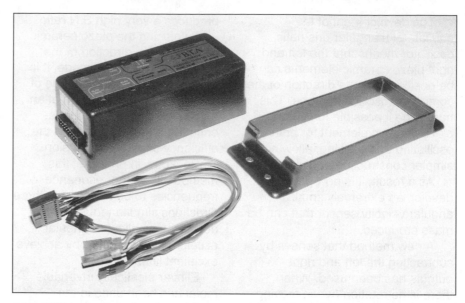

*The BTA autopilot, developed from a unit used for military purposes, can be operated in large-scale models to give smoother and more accurate flying.*

*Above and opposite: With a BTA autopilot fitted, and a dual frequency radio control system, the 'Schleppi' proved to be exceptionally safe and stable to fly.*

receiver and servos. A spare channel (function) is used for engaging or disengaging the unit during flight. No separate battery supply is needed, but as the unit is continuously running and the gyros and electronics have an average current draw of 100MA, it is prudent to use a larger-capacity

battery for the receiver/servo/ autopilot supply.

With the autopilot disengaged the model will fly normally, but on switching in the autopilot and centralising the control sticks, the model will recover to a straight and level situation, providing that the unit has been trimmed to coincide

with the trim of the model. With the autopilot engaged the control movements of the aileron and elevator are reduced (similar to the rates being switched in), but leave sufficient control for safe flying. The control inputs are adjustable.

Using the autopilot in conjunction with a PCM fail-safe would certainly improve the chances of minimising damage to the model in the event of a radio interference. When the fail-safe comes into operation the controls would be programmed for the engine to cut, the rudder set to neutral (or slight left turn – experience would determine the position) and the autopilot would provide a low bank left-hand turn and, probably, slight up elevator.

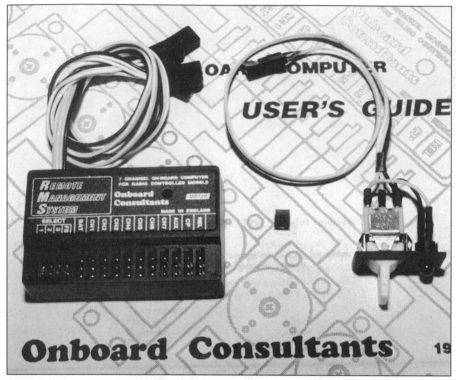

*Fitting a Remote Management System between the receiver and the servos of an FM standard radio system will provide many of the options available on higher-specification outfits.*

The aim here would be to achieve a steady left-hand gliding turn, which would be achievable, via the autopilot, even with inherently unstable models.

Because the BTA autopilot contains gyros and electronics it is a relatively bulky unit; no doubt advancements in solid state gyros allied to micro-processors will result in smaller units in the future.

There are applications for such products in scale model flying, helicopters and certainly for training purposes where, if the student gets into problems, it only needs the flick of a switch to recover the model.

Gyro-operated autopilots are not the only way to go. Ready to come on to the market is an autopilot for three functions – elevator and one or two aileron servos – that works through an external visual sensor picking up the 'light and shade' conditions on the horizon. This system promises to give good results with an aeroplane under power or on the glide, and will recover an inverted model. The cost of this small and lightweight unit should be considerably less than the gyro autopilot.

For the modeller who has purchased a basic radio control outfit, then realises that he needs the facilities of a more complex system, this does not mean that he must buy a complete new system. By making use of a micro-processor, some clever electronics and an equally clever switching arrangement, it is possible to use an add-on unit to give facilities that would only be found in up-market radio systems.

RMS operates with non-PCM systems, plugs into the four basic function outputs of the receiver and gives the potential for programming options such as the following:

Seven channels
Servo throw adjustment
Servo neutral adjustment
Servo 'end point' adjustment
Exponential on all channels
Universal mixing
Fail-safe
Interference suppression
Two-servo differential drive
Nicad monitoring
Glitch counting
Glo-plug driver
Two-model memory

All this from a basic four-, five- or six-function FM radio? Yes, with the proviso that the functions have to be programmed into the RMS before flight and cannot be switched or varied during operation. It is also limited, obviously, by the control sticks, switches and sliders that you have on the transmitter, so that, for instance, if you have pre-selected elevator/flap mixing it cannot be switched out during flight.

Some of the other clever things it can do are allowing you to move the throttle servo without even switching on the transmitter – I do not know of another system that offers this feature – and providing a 'system on' warning device where there is an audible bleep from the unit if the transmitter controls have not been operated for 3 minutes.

Whether such add on devices will continue in production will depend on the advances in 'Entry level' radio outfits and the comparative costs.

## Automatic overkill

There comes a point when the use of too many 'automatic' features, such as snap rolls, landing

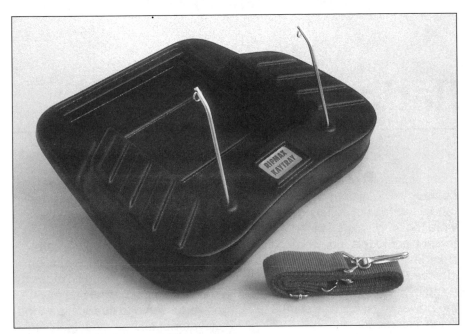

*Transmitter trays are available for those modellers who find it more comfortable supporting the transmitter in this way.*

*The Ripmax HAL 2100 (Horizontal Auto Levelling system) operates with an optical sensor unit receiving light from four quarters as the plane is flying. Because of the ability of it to maintain the model in straight and level flight a fail-safe radio should be fitted.*

letting go. From there on the model would take off, carry out the planned manoeuvres, return to the circuit and – providing that there had not been any major wind changes, automatically land. With the new satellite-linked, fabulously accurate navigation aids, which will pinpoint your position to a matter of metres, it might be possible to incorporate such a device, then even wind velocity would not be a problem.

A marvellous technical achievement, but quite contrary to the reasons for having radio control in the first place. Radio control is there to enable *us* to make the model do what *we* want it to, and when we want it to. Electronic 'aids' should be there to enable us to carry out these functions more efficiently – not to take over control completely!

## Carrying aids

Finally, on a more mundane level, there are a few accessories to make our operations more comfortable and safer. Neck straps, either in conjunction with a transmitter tray, or just the tray, are obtainable as accessories. For cold conditions it is essential to keep your hands warm, for your fingers are carrying out intricate and delicate manoeuvres on the transmitter, and for this purpose a transmitter 'mitt' is a most sensible addition to the normal cold weather clothing.

We should always strive to keep our equipment in the best of order and a little cosseting would not go amiss. Transmitter carrying cases, similar to aluminium camera cases, are available from R/C manufacturers and independent suppliers; they will keep your equipment dry, warm, clear of dirt – and prying fingers!

attitude, gyro stabilisation, autopilots (and I am sure that there are lots still to come), becomes self-defeating. For example, it is just about feasible to have a tape, or disk, with a program of a flight that could be inserted in a computerised transmitter. With the addition of such data as the prevailing wind velocity, altitude of the take-off and landing area and the runway direction, it would then be a matter of pointing the model down the runway, with the engine(s) running, starting the program on the transmitter and

# Chapter 4

# Radio Installations

Certain radio control equipment installations will be geared to all types of models, but some are specific to the particular types. The specifics will be dealt with in the chapter relating to the different classes of models, while this chapter will explain the general principles and investigate the different types of servos.

## Operating environments

The environments in which our radio equipment will have to operate will vary enormously according to the model type. An off- road IC-engine-powered racing car will have to suffer the vibrations from the engine, the thumps and bangs of traversing a rough track, possibly water and inevitably being rolled over and unceremoniously thumped back on to its wheels. A scale model boat, on the other hand, will be sailed serenely, is not likely to be involved in any bone-crunching shunts and, with electric power, will not be subjected to high vibration levels, but may suffer from getting wet.

Many years ago, when radio equipment was less reliable than it is now, a model glider pilot commented on the number of failures the power flyers were having compared with himself. He was convinced that either we were using the wrong equipment, installing it badly or were just poor flyers. The true reason was much

more simple, if not immediately obvious to the glider pilot. With his model he was not suffering the vibration levels experienced with the power models, nor were the linkages and servos being stressed by energetic aerobatic flying of the type undertaken by the power boys; his was sedate flying in comparison.

Vibration is the enemy of R/C equipment, especially for electro-mechanical devices, and the failures of the power models were mostly related to this and the strains on the servos. Equipment has improved since those days and is not as susceptible to vibration, servos are more powerful and nicad batteries more

consistently reliable. This is, however, not an excuse for poor installations – it is still more than possible to have a radio failure as a direct result of not taking care with the planning and installation of the equipment – and linkages. There is no point in having a powerful servo to operate, say, the elevator of a large model, only to lose half the power through bad linkages and hinging of the control surface.

## Planning the installation

Model helicopters, cars, some boats, and ARTF (Almost Ready To Fly) aeroplanes will have instructions that state and illustrate

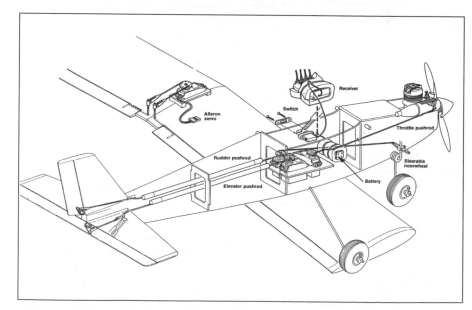

*A typical R/C installation for high-wing or shoulder-wing models (with acknowledgment to Thunder Tiger).*

## LINKAGE OF PITCH CONTROL

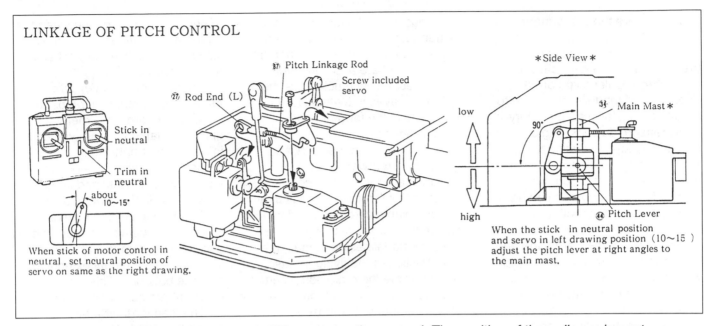

㊲ Pitch Linkage Rod

㉗ Rod End (L)

Screw included servo

Stick in neutral

Trim in neutral

about 10~15°

When stick of motor control in neutral , set neutral position of servo on same as the right drawing.

*Side View*

low / high

90°

㉞ Main Mast *

㊹ Pitch Lever

When the stick in neutral position and servo in left drawing position (10~15 ) adjust the pitch lever at right angles to the main mast.

*Two steps taken from a Kyosho electric helicopter instruction manual. The position of the radio equipment, gyro and speed controller are all predetermined and linkages are provided.*

## INSTALLATION OF THE RECEIVER/GYRO AND SWITCH

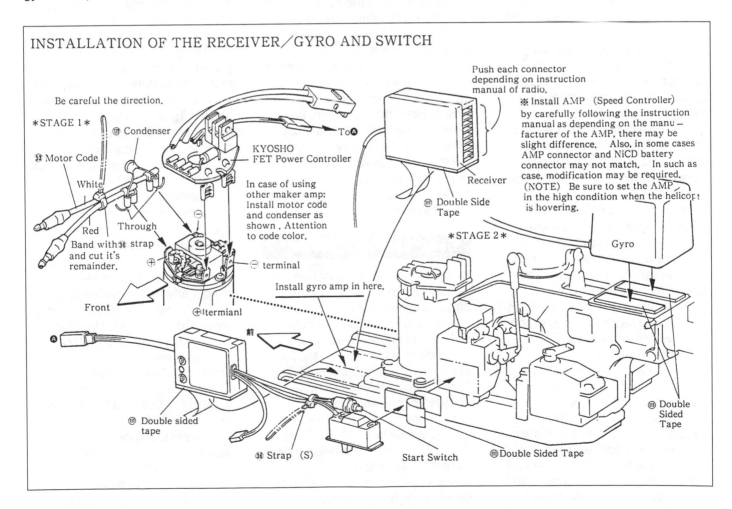

Push each connector depending on instruction manual of radio.

※Install AMP (Speed Controller) by carefully following the instruction manual as depending on the manu – facturer of the AMP, there may be slight difference. Also, in some cases AMP connector and NiCD battery connector may not match. In such as case, modification may be required. (NOTE) Be sure to set the AMP in the high condition when the helicort is hovering.

Be careful the direction.

*STAGE 1*

㉒ Condenser

㊵ Motor Code

White

Red

Through

Band with㊱ strap and cut it's remainder.

Front

KYOSHO FET Power Controller

In case of using other maker amp: Install motor code and condenser as shown . Attention to code color.

⊖ terminal

⊕ termianl

Install gyro amp in here.

To Ⓐ

Receiver

⑩ Double Side Tape

*STAGE 2*

Gyro

Ⓐ

⑩ Double sided tape

㊱ Strap (S)

Start Switch

⑩ Double Sided Tape

⑪ Double Sided Tape

exactly where the component parts of the radio equipment are to go. In this case follow the instructions precisely and carefully, checking at each stage. Unless you are a very experienced modeller and wish to modify the installation for a very good reason, do stick religiously to the installation instructions, keeping to the specific sequence, or you may find that you are unable to fit some part if you have gone your own way with the assembly order.

For many of the aeroplane and boat designs built from plans you will, to a large extent, be on your own with the installation of the radio equipment. There may be some general positions indicated, but it will be your responsibility to work out the precise positioning of the items and how they are linked to the control surfaces.

Accessibility is an obvious requirement with regard to the installed equipment; we may need to get to it for future servicing, or to change an item. One of the few times that a component is 'built in' is with the aileron servo of a contest glider, or a scale model aeroplane, in the first instance for maximum efficiency and in the second the need not to have any visible access panels. In these instances, if a servo does fail, the structure has to be cut away for it to be replaced. There should be no problems of accessibility in model boats, cars and helicopters where large hatches are available, or the whole of the body shells can be removed.

The balance of a model, fore and aft, is important and is more critical in an aircraft than it is in a boat (aeroplanes crash from greater heights!). The exact point of balance will not be known until the model is finished and checked, and you are lucky if it comes out exactly as shown on the model

drawings. If at all avoidable it is better not to have to carry ballast in the form of dead weight; there is one proviso here and that is that the correct balance point must be achieved, even if, eventually, it has to be in the form of dead weight ballast.

To try to fly a model with, for instance, a rearward centre of gravity (balance point) is courting disaster; it will probably result in an uncontrollable aeroplane and you will be left not knowing whether it was the model design at fault, the construction or the flying. Please do not blame the radio equipment – if you carried out your pre-flight checks properly, it is most unlikely to be the R/C equipment that is at fault.

Adjustment of the balance point can be made by moving the internal weight distribution around, so if some of the heavier components can be movable it will help to achieve the correction without resorting to added ballast. The obvious movable item, and probably the heaviest and most effective, is the battery; indeed, unless you have no alternative but to position it in one place, the battery should be considered as a movable item.

## Battery installation

Because it is the heaviest item, the battery is also the most likely to cause damage in a crash. Partially for this reason, but also to help isolate it from engine vibrations, the pack should be protected by enclosing it in a resilient material. Foam plastic, unless of high density, is useless as a protector of batteries – it will not have sufficient resistance to crushing. Some of the domestic heating pipe insulation, available from DIY stores or plumbers' merchants, is satisfactory, but you can test the

material by pressing it between the thumb and forefinger; if it shows little resistance it will not act as a shock absorber.

Foam rubber is an excellent material for containing the battery, either in the form of carpet underlay material or the type used in cushions or upholstery (note rubber, not plastic). The battery should be fully contained in the foam. If it is in the form of a long pack (four pen cells tag-welded together in a vertical format), the pack can be slipped into a foam tube, with the material extending past the batteries. This will give sufficient protection all round.

The lead for the battery normally extends from one end of the pack, and although this may be trapped by the plastic covering, or box, it is advisable to further restrain it. Battery packs do often have to go into 'hard-to-get-at' places, and there is a temptation to pull the battery by the lead, with a risk of straining the joint on the battery. To avoid this, either double back the existing lead on to the pack and tape securely, or make a separate string or tape loop to pull on when removing the battery.

Wherever the battery is finally positioned, ensure that it is secure and unlikely to damage anything immediately in front of it in a crash. To place the battery immediately behind the receiver, or servos, without any further restraint, such as a bulkhead, is a bad economic policy. Receivers and servos cost more than batteries to replace.

If the battery is to be placed in a position where it may be contaminated by oil (for example, in the same bay as a fuel tank) or water, it should be wrapped in a heavyweight polythene bag, the neck sealed with a rubber band and silicone rubber.

It is possible to make up your own receiver battery pack from

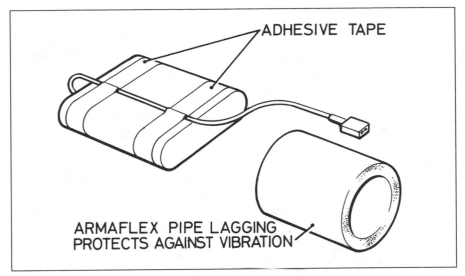

ADHESIVE TAPE

ARMAFLEX PIPE LAGGING
PROTECTS AGAINST VIBRATION

*Battery leads should be restrained and the pack well insulated and protected by a crush-resistant foam material.*

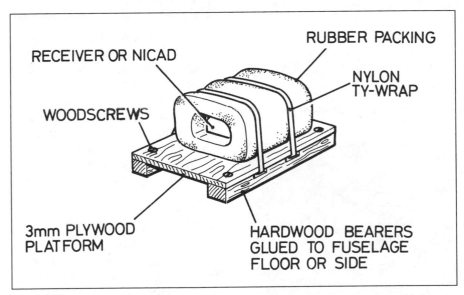

RECEIVER OR NICAD

RUBBER PACKING

NYLON
TY-WRAP

WOODSCREWS

3mm PLYWOOD
PLATFORM

HARDWOOD BEARERS
GLUED TO FUSELAGE
FLOOR OR SIDE

*The battery or receiver can be securely positioned on a plywood platform, providing that this is readily accessible.*

single nicad cells, although this is normally unnecessary unless you want to use more or less than four cells. If you do wire the cells together yourself, make certain the contacts are clean, and use a substantial high-wattage soldering iron to make the connections; prolonged heat on nical cells can permanently damage the battery. The use of battery boxes is not to be recommended as they are electrically much inferior to a welded pack.

As previously stated, nicads put up with an awful amount of punishment without complaint, but they are your only source of power for the equipment – unless you have a back-up pack. You may find that you have inadvertently allowed the cell voltage to go below the recommended 1.1 volts and the charger will no longer charge up the pack. It is possible to give them a 'boost charge', possibly from a quick charger, to get the process started, then charge as normal. In this case, and all instances when you have doubts about the battery pack, put it through a cycler and note the charge and operational life; it will tell you whether it is still good.

Sometimes just one cell of a pack can be damaged, and you may get a false impression when the equipment is first tested. The initial post-charge voltage per cell might be as high as 1.4 volts, and although this does not last long, three good cells may give sufficient voltage to operate your equipment – for a short period. If in any real doubt about the condition of nicad batteries, in the transmitter or receiver or for servo operation, throw them away – it could save you a lot of money.

## On/off switch

Normally of the slide variety (toggle switches are too easily switched off accidentally, unless they are of the protected type), they are of the double pole type for additional security. I suppose in the reliability stakes – which item of model-borne R/C equipment is most likely to fail – the switch would come second, after the servos and before the receiver and battery; by far the most likely cause of a crash is, and will always remain, operational error.

Switches can fail because of the strain placed on the wires soldered to them, but more likely due to dirty or worn contacts. If we can keep the switch out of the way of engine exhaust deposits, general dirt and dust from the operation area and – the nastiest of all enemies to radio equipment – water (even worse, salt water), then we will be doing ourselves a favour.

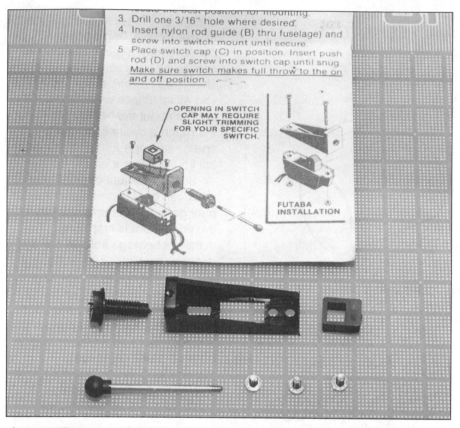

*A remotely operated switch will keep it clear of dirt and exhaust residues.*

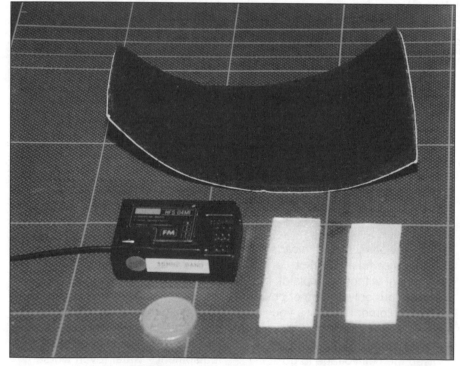

*The Hitec four-channel mini-receiver is supplied complete with resilient foam packing and 'Velcro' strips.*

As mentioned in the Ancillaries chapter, it is possible to purchase, quite cheaply, a remote operation unit for the on/off switch. If you cannot purchase one of these it is not too difficult to make a simple wire pull/push arrangement.

No further precautions are necessary to isolate the switch from vibration, although it is sensible to mount it well away from the engine. When the switch has to be mounted on the side of the model, do make sure it is on the side away from the engine silencer outlet! For very large models it is worth considering the use of two switches arranged in parallel.

## Receiver

The most delicate and expensive part of the equipment in the model should come in for some special treatment. Unfortunately the receiver is all too often wedged tightly in an area where it will be offered little protection, either from engine vibration or crash damage.

The same principles of protection apply to the receiver as they did with the battery pack, but fortunately, with less mass to consider, we have a slightly easier task. Light foam plastic is still definitely out, however – the foam should be good and resilient. The receiver should be loosely fitted in its foam 'box' and this in turn should be a loose fit in the model, minimising the risk of transmitted vibration.

Planning your total installation ahead will allow you to position the receiver so that the servo and battery plug sockets are readily accessible and with no risk of straining the leads. If possible the receiver should be mounted vertically in an aeroplane fuselage; in this position there is less risk of printed circuit board components being 'bent-over' in a sudden-stop accident (not a problem with SMT

– Surface Mounted Technology). Remember, too, that you may wish to change the frequency crystal, but the receiver should be easily accessible, anyway.

In R/C cars, where space for equipment is at a premium, the receiver is often fitted directly to the chassis by using nylon tie-wraps. This is not the ideal mounting for a receiver as it will have little protection from directly transmitted vibration. Even a thin pad of resilient foam will help to reduce vibration levels, and SMT receivers will be better equipped to cope with shock loads.

## Aerials

Receiver aerials are a necessary evil, and although there may be a temptation to cut one short, or to partially coil the aerial inside the model, this must never be done; a serious reduction in radio range will certainly be the result. Aerials should be directly routed outside the model as soon as possible and be kept clear of battery and switch leads. Leave a certain amount of slack on the aerial between the receiver and where it exits the model, and provide some positive means of preventing the aerial/servo connection from being strained, if it is accidentally pulled from the outside. The aerial is then routed to some suitable location on the model, a mast or the fin, and secured by returning the very end of the aerial back into a piece of plastic tubing and retaining it with a small rubber band.

Boats and cars may well use whip aerials, or a vertical arrangement of the standard receiver aerial, and this is quite adequate for the short operating distances for these models. Whip aerials have gone out of fashion for model aeroplanes; they were almost obligatory in the early days when signal strengths were lower and it was important to get every bit of the transmitted signal to the receiver.

Although signal range is rarely a problem, there are times when the whip aerial still has a distinct advantage, particularly when flying very large models. The manufacturer's instruction manual may well give a warning not to point the transmitter antenna (aerial) directly towards the model. However, if the model is taking off in front of you, the favoured position, and the aerial on the model is taken from the fuselage back to the fin, you have the potential for the least favourable transmitting and receiving condition. It is all too easy to let the transmitter antenna drop a little (particularly with a 'straight-out-of-the-top' aerial) and with a large model disappearing rapidly into the distance the received signal will inevitably be weak. A whip, vertical, model aerial would be a boon in such instances.

## Plugs and sockets

Receivers normally feature a block connector for direct plugging of the servos and battery. Some will have the sixth or seventh channel (function) as a fly lead into which can be plugged the battery and the extra function, allowing the connection to be made without having to remove the receiver from its protective sleeve; this sleeve also helps to retain the servo plugs in their receiver sockets.

Separate plugs and sockets, such as extension leads and battery harnesses, should be checked for plug security, and if there is any looseness, the plug and socket should be taped together, with electrical adhesive tape, to ensure that they will not work loose. Extension leads, for instance for the aileron servo, should always be used where otherwise there would be a danger of straining the servo lead. An all too regular sight is a modeller, with the wing of his aeroplane resting

*Installation is complete except for the routing of the aerial, which should be restrained internally then routed outside the fuselage to the fin. The receiver is mounted on rubber pads.*

*All the major manufacturers have a wide range of servos to augment their outfits. They range from the micro servo, weighing as little as 12g, to the giant quarter-scale monsters with high outputs and needing a separate power source.*

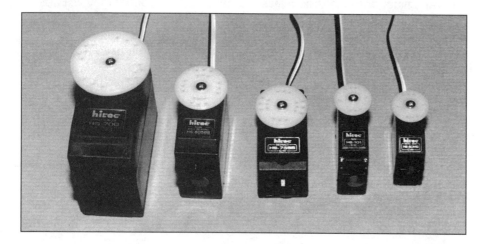

on the fuselage, tugging at the aileron servo lead to make it reach the receiver; an extension lead would obviate this straining. Many R/C outfits include a servo extension lead; if yours does not, go out and buy one – it will be used.

## Servos

The choice of servos supplied by manufacturers of R/C outfits and other independent suppliers is vast, and often confusing to the newcomer to radio control. Why should there be such a variety? I have just counted 20 different types by one manufacturer, and that is without any specialist boat servos.

With most outfits aimed at the beginner, where costs are at a premium in a very competitive market, 'standard' servos are included in the set, and they will be of moderate size with plain bearings (typically 34 mm high, 19 mm wide and 39 mm long, weighing 45 g). Many experienced modellers will denigrate the use of these servos, but for general sports models they are perfectly adequate. To qualify this statement, a flying training scheme I was involved with had two training models (with 'buddy box' systems fitted) and standard

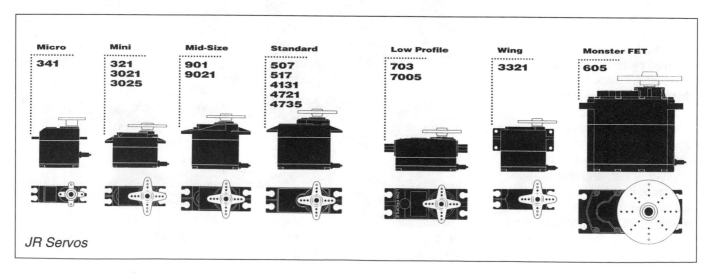

*JR Servos*

*Manufacturer's 'standard' servos, as normally supplied with a radio control outfit, should not be denigrated. They are capable of giving reliable service and sufficient accuracy for most modellers. The exploded view shows the construction of a standard, non-ballraced servo, the Futaba S148.*

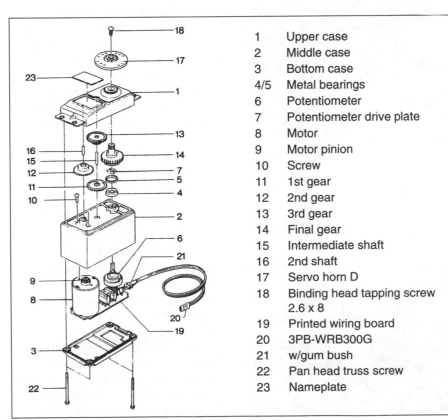

| 1 | Upper case |
|---|---|
| 2 | Middle case |
| 3 | Bottom case |
| 4/5 | Metal bearings |
| 6 | Potentiometer |
| 7 | Potentiometer drive plate |
| 8 | Motor |
| 9 | Motor pinion |
| 10 | Screw |
| 11 | 1st gear |
| 12 | 2nd gear |
| 13 | 3rd gear |
| 14 | Final gear |
| 15 | Intermediate shaft |
| 16 | 2nd shaft |
| 17 | Servo horn D |
| 18 | Binding head tapping screw 2.6 x 8 |
| 19 | Printed wiring board |
| 20 | 3PB-WRB300G |
| 21 | w/gum bush |
| 22 | Pan head truss screw |
| 23 | Nameplate |

servos were installed in these models. They have been performing for three years, have survived numerous crashes and had many hours of operation; during this time only one servo gave any problem, when it started to go slow (perhaps as a protest at the treatment it was receiving!).

The need for micro, the smallest, and miniature servos is fairly obvious, and these are available in standard form, with metal gear trains and ballrace outputs. For the average modeller, just wishing to fly a small electric model, the standard micro or miniature servo may be satisfactory, but contest glider pilots, racing car enthusiasts and operators of any model where there are likely to be higher loads on the servos would be well advised to opt for the more expensive ballraced, metal-geared variety. These may give greater accuracy, stand shock loads better, but may wear more rapidly.

Miniature, as opposed to micro, servos specifically designed for electric buggy cars will have high torque, high speed, double-ballraced features to cope with the requirements of accuracy, rapid reaction (0.19 seconds for 60 degrees travel is typical) and high servo output (over 5 kg/cm). Sailplane pilots may not be looking for the same outputs, where there is one servo per aileron, but are more interested in relatively light weights and good resolution.

For the advanced modeller, looking for rather more output and speed than is provided by the standard servo, there is usually a choice of high-torque, single- or double-ballraced types, with or without cored motors. These will have outputs ranging from around 3.0 to 4.0 kg/cm torque and speeds of 0.25 seconds per 60 degrees movement, or better.

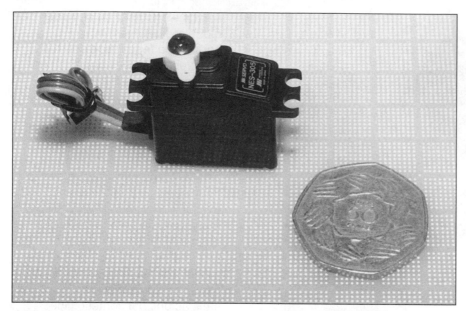

*Micro servos – and receivers and batteries – allow ever smaller models to be built and operated. Although two types of aeroplanes are illustrated here (below and opposite), the micro systems also have their uses in cars and boats.*

In addition to the normal operation servos, where they return to a neutral position, there are also servos with movements from one end of the travel to the opposite end, ie not proportional. These are usually referred to as retract servos (used, typically, for raising and lowering under-carriages) and are available in single- or double-ballraced versions and, sometimes, in a low-profile layout for easier installation within the wing thickness. There are, of course, other uses for retract servos, and the gearing will give higher torque outputs at the expense of speed.

Competition aerobatic and helicopter pilots will be looking for the highest quality, high-speed, high-torque servos with the best resolution possible. This is particularly important for the latest '3D' (free aerobatics) helicopter flying where instant response is essential, the model being flown near to the ground in every conceivable manoeuvre. For the aerobatic pilot, too, it is necessary to have high standards of servo response and precision; he is looking for absolute repeatability. These pilots are catered for with a good variety of precision ballraced servos, albeit at an extra cost, which will have the latest electronic technology and high-performance, minimum dead band, coverless motors.

With many modellers now going for 'giant'-size models, particularly in aircraft, but increasingly also with vehicles, the manufacturers have found it necessary to introduce servos to cope with the extra loads generated in these models. Naturally these are larger and heavier than the standard-size servos if both very high torque and good speed (comparable to other servos) are to be achieved and

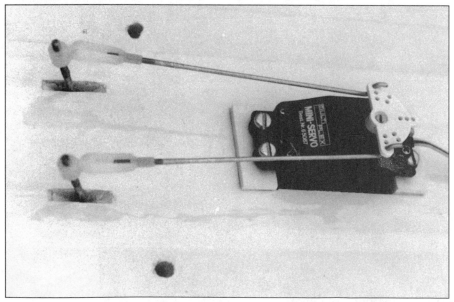

*Mini-servos are useful for aileron installations, both for torque rod operation and individual ailerons where the servo has to be buried in the wing.*

qualities maintained. Though not essential, it is prudent to provide a separate battery supply for these 'giant' servos (sometimes referred to as 'quarter scale'), and it may be advantageous to increase the voltage to 6, or even 8.4, volts – check with the manufacturer's instructions.

No doubt manufacturers will continue in their quest to improve servo standards and to introduce new designs as they become necessary. A closer look at presently available servos will give a closer insight into this most important electro-mechanical device – the muscle of the outfit.

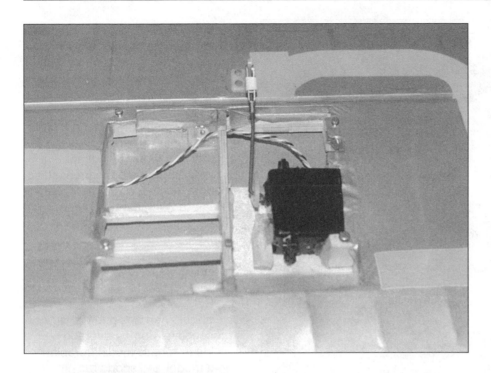

or electronically inclined modeller to take a servo apart – you are unlikely to get it back together in working order.

As described before, the receiver sends the decoded signal to the individual servo and this informs the servo of the required position of the output shaft – to which is connected the feedback 'pot'. If the position of the output shaft does not match the signal requirements, the shaft is moved until the two coincide. When this situation is achieved the electric motor switches off and the servo output remains static until a new signal is received.

## 'Expert' or 'standard'?

The basic workings of the servo are the same for all types, so why the variations, not the least in terms of cost where you may be able to buy 20 'standard' servos for the price of a single large-output servo?

Requirements for accuracy, speed and power are the reasons put forward by the manufacturers for the extra cost of the 'expert' ranges of servos. This will entail the inclusion of high-quality electric motors, ballraced outputs, precision gear chains and advanced electronics. How far the additional costs are justified is for you to decide, but there is no doubt that the modern radio control transmitters and receiver/decoders can make full use of the most accurate and fastest servos available.

The standard form of three- or five-pole Ferrite electric motor, hardly changed throughout the century, consists of a central rotating armature and the outer, magnetic section, which provides the rotating force. It is the wire-wound armature that presents the problems for real accuracy in the servo; the inertia produced makes

## Servo selection

Consisting of an electric motor, gear train, feedback 'pot' (potentiometer), electronic

amplifier, case and output device (arm or disc), the servo is quite a compact bundle of activity. So much so that I would not recommend the non-mechanical

*The latest 'super' servos feature coreless electric motors, no backlash gear chains, ballraced outputs, zero dead band and high speed and torque.*

it more difficult to stop the rotation and to reverse the movement. We may only be talking about weights of a gram or two, but this is sufficient to inhibit the last few percentages of accuracy.

More commonly used in higher-priced servos are the coreless motors that feature a hollow armature with the permanent static magnet located inside the armature. With a much lower rotating mass, the acceleration and deceleration speeds are improved, centring torque is higher, there is less overshoot and the overall resolution is improved.

Before we get too carried away we should perhaps put this in perspective. For the average sports aerobatic model aeroplane, boat model and sports racing vehicle, it is very unlikely that the operator would notice any difference in the control of the model, whether fitted with the 'expert' or 'standard' servos. Other factors, such as linkages, hinges – and operating skills – are likely to outweigh any improvements in servo accuracy or speed.

## Feedback 'pots'

These are sealed units and, for maximum accuracy, are fixed to the output shaft and are not adjustable (older servos often had a small screw for centre adjustment accessed under the output disc). Where the servo is advertised as having a 'remote pot', the feedback 'pot' is not fixed to the output shaft and is gear driven. The advantage with this arrangement is the reduced effect of vibration and shock, and servos of this type are particularly useful for off-road cars and any models subject to high vibration levels.

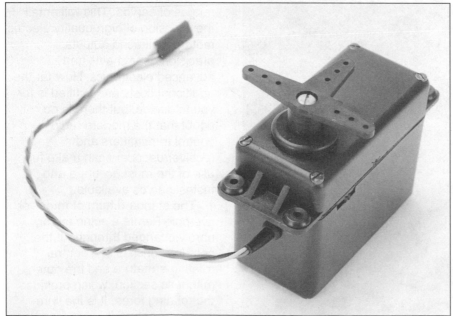

*An early 'giant' servo was produced in kit form; it had a trim adjustment on the side of the case.*

*Micro and Mammoth – the size difference in the range of commercial servos is well illustrated by the Union Ultra Micro compared to the Hitec 'Quarter Scale' servo. The other views show details of the latter's workings.*

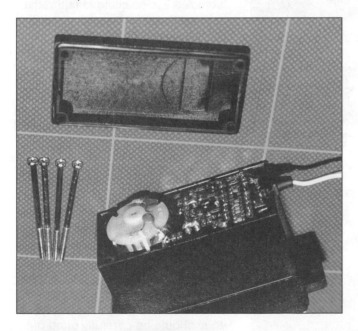

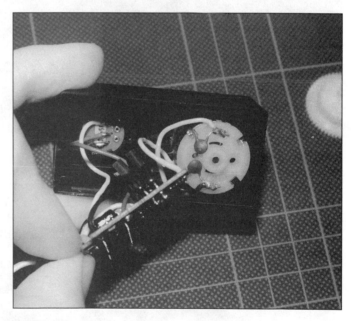

## Gear trains

Whether moulded plastic or metal, gear trains are normally strong enough for their designed purposes, and it is only when the shock loads on the gears are higher than expected, that failures are likely to occur. In a crash something will break, and perhaps it is better to lose a couple of teeth from a nylon gear, or a broken output arm, than to damage some other component that will be more expensive to replace.

With regard to the comparative accuracy of moulded nylon or metal gear wheels, there is probably little difference; both systems will give a high degree of precision. One area where it is advisable to consider the use of metal gears is with micro or mini servos. Because of the small overall dimensions of the servo the gear trains also have to be miniaturised, and the moulded gears may be too thin to take any substantial shock loads – as may be experienced from an off-road electric-powered vehicle.

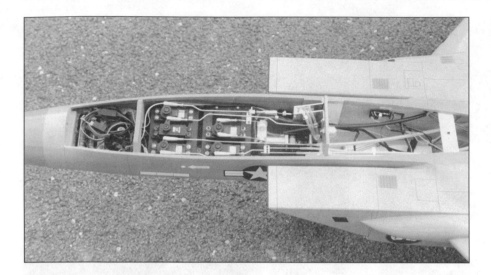

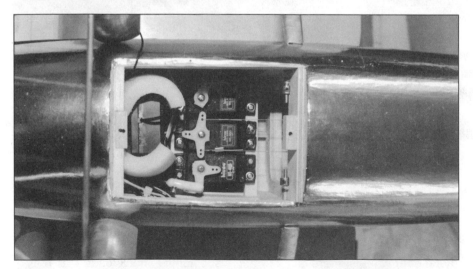

*Where space for the radio equipment is limited, good pre-planning is essential, and this includes selecting servos that will fit into the available space and be right for the job. With cramped installations the advantages of having the full electronic adjustments are not to be underestimated.*

## Ballraces

These are also a common feature of up-market servos. The alternative is to have a plastic bush bearing, which will wear in conditions of high use and rough operation (dust, fuel, water and vibration). High-output shaft side-loads, as may be experienced with direct connection, closed-loop control systems, warrant the use of dual-ballraced servos, and the higher loads involved in large models and 'mega' servos are also cases for the ballraced versions. Wherever possible the shock loads, from a steerable nose or tail wheel for instance, should be isolated from the servo and link via an intermediate control crank. For vehicles it is possible to fit throttle and brake over-ride and steering 'servo savers' to reduce the risk of damage to the servos as a result of shock loads transmitted through the linkage.

## Servo performance

Contamination, in the form of dust, fuel and water, is most likely to occur to the servos fitted in R/C cars. Some servos are made more resistant to these elements by using rubber, or soft plastic, seals to the case joints and tight fitting grommets to the exit wire leads. However, this does not make them truly waterproof, and if they do become completely submerged they should be carefully dried out.

Given the same electric motor in a variety of servos, the characteristics of the servos will basically be a compromise between speed and torque. You can either have a very fast-moving output, measured in seconds per degree arc, with a modest output torque, measured in kilograms at 1cm from the centre of the output device; or the opposite, where the

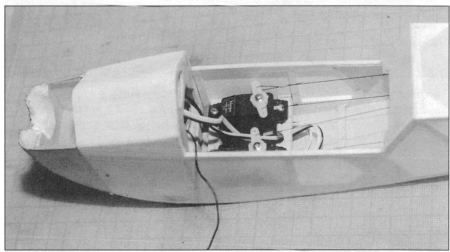

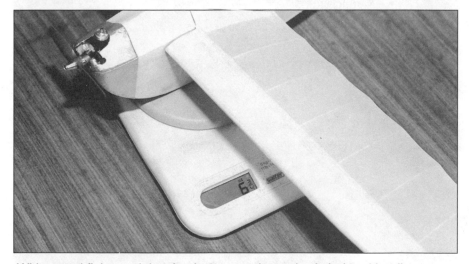

*With a total flying weight of only 6¾ ozs, the author's indoor Handley Page Sayer model has micro servos, a 50mAh battery and miniature receiver. To minimise weight, a closed-loop, nylon monofilament cable, control linkage is used.*

torque is high and the speed relatively slow. The 'standard' would be somewhere in between.

As examples, a 'standard' servo with a three-pole Ferrite motor, direct-drive 'pot' and no ballrace may give a torque of 3kg/cm and a speed of 0.25sec/60 degrees, while the higher-performance servo (of similar dimensions and only marginally heavier) will provide 6.5kg/cm torque and a rotation speed of 0.15sec/60 degrees. This represents quite a difference in torque and speed, but this is only relevant if the model being operated requires these higher specifications.

'Dead band' is a term used in relation to high-performance servos, and 'zero dead band' is the aim for maximum accuracy in centring. With a wide dead band the motor is not constantly hunting to keep the servo accurately centred, but will give a 'slack' resolution and exact centring will not take place. Going to the other extreme, if a genuine zero dead band is to be achieved, the servo motor will be almost constantly moving clockwise and anti-clockwise to attain that final degree (or, more to the point, minute) of accuracy. Current drains with the higher-performance servos usually have considerably higher current draw in the idle and operating conditions.

Different shapes, for example low-profile or wing-mounted, make up some of the other servo variations, plus the non-centring end-to-end movement types used for retractable undercarriages.

As previously mentioned it is often other considerations such as poor linkages that have more effect on control accuracy. Another factor that is rarely considered is whether the full movement of the servo is being employed. With modern micro-computer transmitters it is a simple matter to reduce the servo travel to any percentage of the full travel – just dial it in! Thus we may only be using 50 per cent of the total available travel, and less than that if low rates are switched in. If we were looking for increased servo speed this would be a good ploy, as the time taken for the servo to move from one extreme to the other would be substantially reduced. In terms of control accuracy the results are the opposite; if there is a given amount of 'wasted' linkage movement over a full servo travel, this unwanted movement will effectively double with the reduced servo travel. To illustrate this problem mechanically, try fitting the control linkages to the outermost point on a control horn, then to that closest to the hinge point, and see which gives the most accurate movement; it will be the one with the linkage connection at the furthest point from the hinge line. In effect, this results from the full movement of the servo being employed.

As you become more experienced in R/C modelling you will begin instinctively to know which servo to fit for certain purposes. No great power is needed to operate the engine throttle arm, for example, nor is speed at an absolute premium (engine and throttle response being much greater factors). Elevators create heavy air loads and power is needed for larger models, without sacrificing too much speed. Ailerons need to be fast-moving, and when a servo is fitted for each aileron, torque can be sacrificed to speed. Just remember that if you are using mixed controls, as with a 'V tail' configuration, the servos should be of the same type so that operating speeds are similar.

Large-scale sailplanes will produce quite high control surface loads and it is important to use servos with adequate output torque. This is particularly so where the ailerons are operated from a centrally mounted servo, as is the case with this 'Rhönsperber'. The rubber band is only to retain the top hatch.

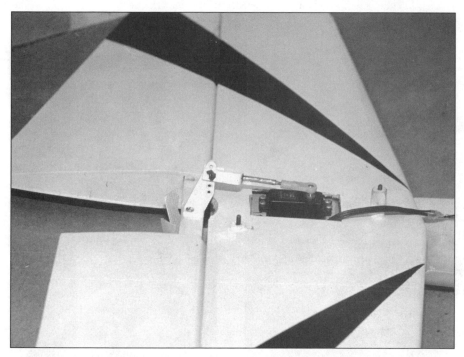

*High-powered, fast and heavy aerobatic radio control models need servos with high torque, high speed and good resolution. To minimise the risk of lost efficiency in the control linkage routes, the servos are mounted at the rear end of the model for elevator and rudder operation. One servo is shown in the tailplane, with a short, direct linkage (ball link to clevis and elevator horn) of suitable proportions. On the other model, belonging to the World Aerobatic Champion, Hanno Prettner, and much flown, the elevator and rudder servos are located at the rear of the fuselage.*

## Servo installation and linkages

There is absolutely no point in having the finest servo, with regards to precision and power, if it is poorly installed, or 'sloppy' linkages and hinges are fitted to the model; it nullifies all that the manufacturer has achieved in producing a first-rate servo. The first essential is to plan the installation of the servos and the linkages. It is no good waiting until the model is complete, then trying to fit in the servos and linkages; this will prove to be a disaster.

Servos need to be installed where they can be fitted easily, with good access to the output arms or discs. It may well be necessary to make some adjustments at the servo output, even with the fully computerised outfit. Linkages can produce unwanted movement ('slop') and friction, reducing the effective power of the servo. Also, unless the servo can make full and free movement over its travel range (do not forget the extra trim movement, too) there is a risk of stalling the servo and rapidly running down the battery.

Linkages should have a minimum of changes of direction, irrespective of the form of linkages used. Bellcranks will never have 100 per cent precision, as there has to be a small degree of 'play' in the bearings and pushrod connections. Bends in linkage 'snakes' will cause extra friction, and bends in the pushrod ends are liable to flexing and giving unwanted movement.

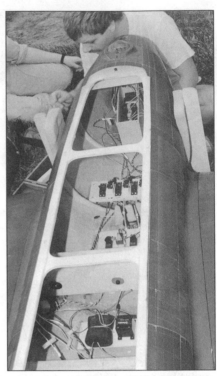

## Fixing the servos

Having designed the installation, including the routes of the linkages, the servos have to be fixed in the model. In an aeroplane it is often logical to fit three servos, operating rudder, elevator and engine throttle, side by side across the fuselage. If the servos are close to one another, it may help with the linkage connections to alternate the direction of the servos (the lead ends). Also, if a closed loop system of control linkage is to be installed for rudder control, the rudder servo should be located in the centre of the servos.

With each servo you will find a mounting system consisting of rubber grommets or pads that fit on to the servo lugs, four eyelets, usually brass, and four fixing screws (micro servos may only have two fixing points). The rubber grommets or pads are slipped on to the ends of the servo lugs, then the eyelets are pushed in from the underside of the holes (the

*For models of this size and importance (the B-17 'Flying Fortresses' were used in the feature film* Memphis Belle*) it is vital that the radio equipment is as near 100 per cent reliable as possible. Fibre optics were utilised between the receivers and servos. Note the bank of switches located in the glazed dome.*

*Typical three-abreast servo installations, one with the output arm locations staggered and the other with a closed-loop rudder control from the centre servo .*

idea, as it will allow the servo to rock more excessively than would be the case with the fore and aft mounting.

Wood-screws are normally supplied for fixing the servos, and these are acceptable if you are fixing to a close-grain hardwood bearer, for example beech or maple. If you are fixing the servos to a plywood plate, it is better to fix them with nuts, bolts and washers. For safety's sake the nuts should be locked in position, either with a lock-nut, Loctite, or a touch of cyanoacrylate adhesive. Absolute security is especially necessary on helicopter models.

Servo mounting trays are provided by some manufacturers in their outfits, but nearly all of them can be obtained as an optional extra. Cars and helicopters will probably have the servo mounting position moulded into the body, but for aeroplanes and boats the servo trays can be a boon. In addition to the trays, normally for three servos, there are also individual servo-mounting brackets, or housings, and these make the installation, and removal, of such things as the aileron servo a lot easier.

The multi servo tray can be fitted to transverse wood bearers or to blocks fitted on the sides of the model. In either case they offer a little more in the way of vibration damping as the trays, in addition to the servos, have a rubber mounting. With some servo trays there are two servos abreast and one transverse. My previous comment regarding reduced precision with this cross-mounting still applies, although this is often for the throttle servo where absolute accuracy is slightly less important.

One other form of servo mounting is to fix the servo to the model structure with servo tape, a dense foam plastic strip with

mounting face). When the servo screws are tightened they can only go as far as the eyelets will allow, thus leaving a chance for the rubber to act as a shock absorber. Do not omit the eyelets, otherwise the screws may be over-tightened on to the rubber and fail to provide any resilience.

Mounting servos is a juggling act between providing a 'soft'

mount, to avoid problems from vibration transmitted from the engine, and not allowing excessive movement of the servo, which will reduce the accuracy of the linkage. For this reason the servos should be mounted fore or aft of the direction of the control linkage; to mount a servo cross-wise to the linkage (except for less important auxiliary controls) is not a good

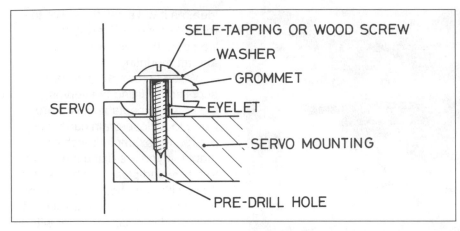

*The correct mounting of a servo into a hardwood bearer.*

adhesive on both sides. There are disadvantages with this system: it is more likely to transmit vibration to the servo and is more likely to come adrift from the structure. I would only recommend servo tape for miniature or micro servos on small models, where space is at a premium. Before fixing the servo in position you must ensure that the surface to which it is to be adhered is clean and impervious; for example, if it is balsa wood it must be treated and sealed with epoxy, dope or resin.

There are a number of 'tricks of the trade' when mounting servos to hardwood rails fixed in the model, not the least of which being pre-planning and careful workmanship. This is a vital part of the model and should not be rushed. For mounting servo trays or servos direct to bearers, ⅜ in sq beech is a very suitable material (½ in sq for large models). The bearer must be securely attached to the model sides, and this is easier, because of the greater surface area, when the bearers are fixed

lengthwise to the sides for the servo tray. For bearers traversing the model structure, a small housing or support must be made for the bearer ends; simply gluing the ends of the bearer to the structure is not good enough. This should all be allowed for at the planning stage and included during construction.

Where the servos are to be directly mounted to the bearers, the spacing of the latter must be precise. They can be pre-drilled, both for the servo screws and for the half-round notches in the centre of the servo fixing, to give clearance for the servo wires where they exit the servo case. Carefully mark the location of the servo's screws and place the two bearers, side by side, in a vice. Make punch marks for the screws and between the bearers at the servo centres; the latter position should be drilled with a 7 or 8 mm (⁵⁄₁₆ in) diameter hole, which will, of course, produce a semi-circular cut-out in each bearer.

Next drill pilot holes for the screws, one size smaller than the diameter of the screw. This will give adequate purchase for the screw without the need for excessive effort. Remove the bearers from the vice and round off the top and lower surfaces of the bearer at the centre positions; this will allow the easy fitting of the servo leads when the servos are installed.

On fitting the servo bearers, double check that the spacing is correct – the ends of the servo case should be just free of the bearers. Use epoxy for gluing the bearers in place, the 1-hour type, or 24-hour type to allow the adhesive to soak well into the wood fibres.

*Mounting servos transversely in the fuselage may lead to a loss of control accuracy due to the rocking action of the servo.*

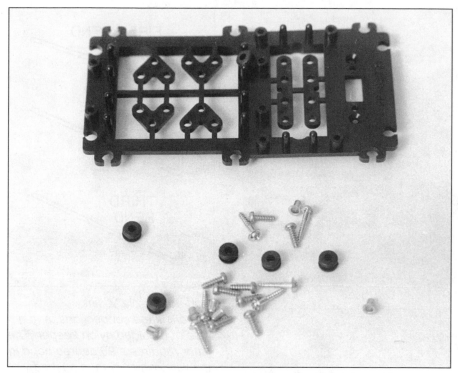

*Servo trays are often designed for two abreast (use for rudder and elevator) and one transverse (throttle). Provision is made for the switch (remotely operated) and rubber grommet shock-absorbing mounting.*

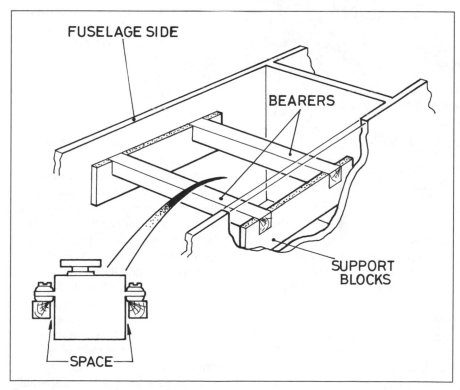

*Hardwood servo bearers need additional support where they are fixed to the fuselage sides.*

## Servo connectors

There are numerous ways of connecting a linkage to the servo output, but the important factor with each is that it must allow smooth movement without friction or strain.

From the earliest days of radio control models, two very simple systems have been used for connecting the linkage, in the form of a pushrod, to the servo output arm.

The first uses a piano wire of suitable gauge (about 1.5 mm diameter, or 16 swg) with a right-angle bend, and a thinner-gauge wire extending under the output disc to act as a retainer.

The second method, the 'Z' link, also uses piano wire, although some modellers prefer to use welding rod, which is a little easier to bend. A 'Z' bend is formed in the end of the wire, either with a special pair of pliers designed for the purpose or by the method illustrated. Making the final action a twisting one makes the forming of the second bend a lot easier. With the 'Z' link the wire must be slipped through the hole in the output arm, or disc, before it is fitted to the servo.

Both of these basic methods have the disadvantage of not being adjustable; any control surface adjustment would have to be made at the other end. However, this may not be a disadvantage as it is unlikely that you will need to make adjustments at both ends, and it may well be more convenient to make the adjustments at the control surface anyway, thus avoiding the removal of hatches or wings. Commercial mouldings are available to achieve the same purpose, and they rely on the pushrod wire being 'snapped' into place.

When it became obvious that R/C modellers would need some

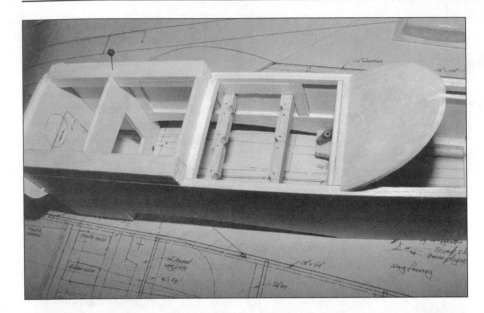

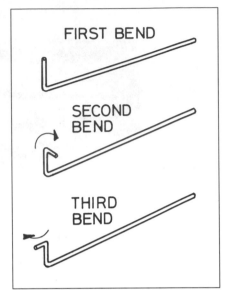

*Non-adjustable 'Z' link servo/linkage connections, and a type of moulded nylon keeper. The latter requires a 90 degree bend in the wire, which is then pushed through the horn or servo arm; the keeper pushes on to the bent end of the wire, and the moulded slot snaps on to the main shaft. It is also possible to use a piece of thin piano wire, soldered to the rod, to take the place of the keeper.*

*Servo bearer positions should be planned before construction commences, then built into the framework. Note that the bearers are pre-drilled for servo screws and leads.*

means of adjusting the overall length of the pushrod, it did not take the accessory manufacturers long to come up with some answers. Probably first on the market was the pressed steel clevis, not a purpose-made article but a component 'purloined' from a typewriter. This works very well, although some of the spring steel versions can be a little vicious to open and have been known to

fracture; a special tool is available to open the jaws of the clevis.

An alternative to this item is the moulded nylon clevis and these can be obtained with a moulded pin or a separate metal pin and in sizes suitable from small models to the largest of designs, where the clevis is vastly stronger than the output of even the mightiest servo. In fact, there is now a whole range of accessories, horns, bellcranks,

etc, specifically designed for large, powerful models.

Both the moulded clevis and pressed steel version are suitable for a threaded-end pushrod; the rod self-taps into the former, while in the latter the thread is already moulded into the clevis. When self-tapping the threaded rod into the clevis you may have to drill out the hole a little, but beware of taking too much out or the threaded rod will not make a strong purchase in the nylon. Conversely, a clevis that can barely be turned is equally poor.

When the above clevises have to be connected to a solid wire, plastic rod or other form of inner cable material, it is necessary to use an adaptor; these are specially manufactured to the particular material and type.

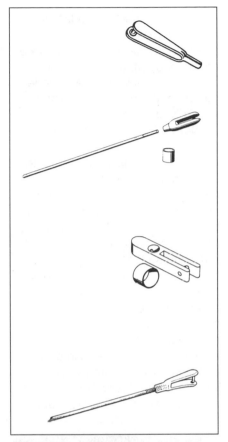

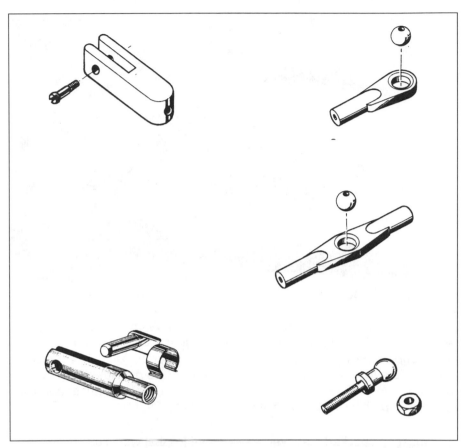

A selection of clevises. The top metal type was the first to be adapted for radio control use – from a typewriter component. The clevis pin locates in a hole in the fork for maximum security. The second drawing shows a metal pin quick link with a threaded rod, while the third illustrates a nylon quick link clevis. Last is a mini snap link with rod. These illustrations of fittings are from Messrs Chart Hobbies.

Many accessories are now obtainable, designed for use on large models where control loads are high. Here we see Chart Hobbies' heavy duty nylon clevis, 25 mm long and 8 mm wide, fitted with a threaded brass clevis pin; a heavy duty metal clevis; a heavy duty ball joint link; a heavy duty double-ended ball link especially useful for aileron and rudder/nose wheel linkages; and finally a threaded ball head stud for fitting to some servo outputs and control horns.

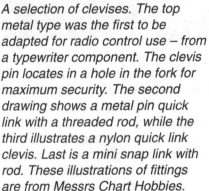

Ball link connectors are suitable for any position where complex movements may be experienced and the angle of connection changes with the movement, for example in helicopters, 'V' tails, car throttle and steering linkages, etc – they are also useful for quick-release servo connections. Single and double swivel socket links are also illustrated.

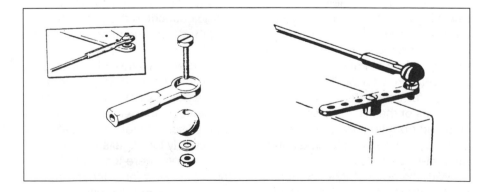

*Multi-engined models need as many back-up systems as possible for reliability and safety. The 'Halifax' in the background has three receivers, one for each side of the aeroplane and one for auxiliary purposes. Each receiver has a main battery and a back-up and the servos have their own power supply. Flying this ⅛th scale beauty, powered by four 62 cc petrol engines, is a two-man operation; one carries out the principal flying, while the co-pilot looks after throttles, undercarriage, flaps and bomb doors. The model was built by Malcolm Gittins, and flown by Paul Heckles.*

It must be checked that over the full movement of the servo output arm there is no binding of the clevis; there is only a certain jaw depth and this must not foul the output. It is particularly important to check this visually, with transmitter trims moved to their full limits, after the servo output has been moved on its spline, to make an adjustment. To ease the problem of binding, and also to give an adjustment of pushrod length, a neat little connector has been devised with a revolving collet fitted on the top of the disc or arm; the wire pushrod end (or Bowden cable) is fed through a horizontal hole then secured with a screw. The only proviso for this system is that the tightness of the retaining screw is checked from time to time; it is probably more suited to small and modest-size models.

With the advent of helicopter models there arose a demand for linkages that would cope with more than just linear movements. For example, in connections between servos and swash plates and in numerous other linkages there were movements in two directions, and standard clevis connectors could not cope with this. Thus the ball joint and swivel socket links were introduced, having of course been used in industry for many years.

Because the cup, or swivel, is moulded, it is connected to a threaded rod and gives provision for adjustment to the pushrod length. Where the pushrod overall length is short, typically on a helicopter, a full threaded rod has a ball joint on each end of the rod. These ball link connectors are not just suitable for helicopters, but are equally suitable for cars, boats and particularly for 'V' tails in aeroplanes where the control movements are non-linear. They can be used for taking up 'difficult'

angles of standard installations, but these may probably have arisen because the installation was not properly planned in the first place. Do check that the threaded portion of the ball component is securely fixed to the servo output.

None of the above devices provide any adjustment of the distance from the servo centre to the output connection, ie the moment arm. Output discs and arms have holes at intervals from the centre to give this adjustment, and the sets of holes may be arranged so that the distances between the holes of the two pairs differ. This gives even more alternatives, and a blank disc in which to drill holes to your own requirements will be included with the servo accessories. An arm with a sliding connector may also be included, and this will give infinite adjustments of the moment arm.

## Special servo installations

In addition to the normal aircraft aileron, elevator, rudder, throttle, flap and undercarriage installations, there are many other uses for servos. They are used to operate valves for smoke systems, parachute dropping, glider-towing releases and bomb drops, to name but a few functions. As we shall see in a forthcoming chapter, they also have many uses in model boats.

With the increasing interest in large-scale models, some well in excess of 50 kg in weight, spanning over 6 metres and powered by engines exceeding 50 cc capacity, ingenuity has to be used to incorporate safety features and to make the best use of existing radio control equipment.

Whereas a standard model aeroplane or helicopter will have one receiver and all the servos

98

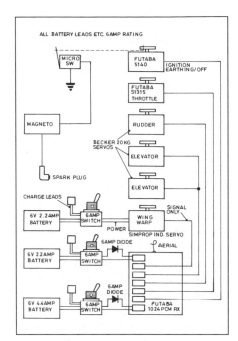

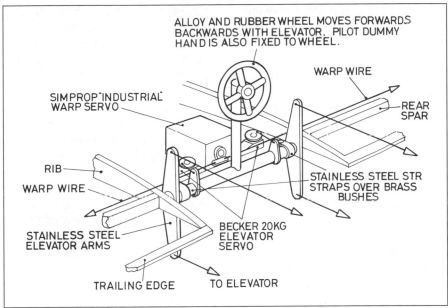

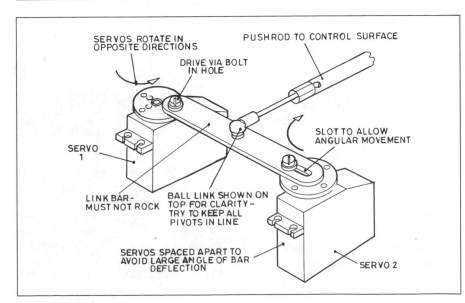

'Twinning' servos.

*For his half-scale Avro Triplane, Ian Turney-White uses a single receiver, with fail-safe, and battery back-up, with a separate battery for the wing-warping servo. No ailerons are fitted and the power required to warp the wings is too much for a normal commercial servo, so an 'Industrial' servo is fitted in its place.*

operating from this, the large models will incorporate different systems. With multi-engine scale models, incorporating many features such as flaps, bomb drops, independent throttle control, etc, one person barely has sufficient hands and fingers to operate all the controls needed! To overcome this difficulty, the control can be split between two transmitters, ie a pilot and co-pilot, as would be the case with the full-size aircraft. The pilot would retain the principal controls of ailerons, elevator and rudder and, with a four-engined model, the inboard engines. The co-pilot would have the responsibility of flap control, outboard engine throttles and all the ancillary features of undercarriage deployment, bomb doors, bomb drops, etc. Obviously this calls for close co-operation between the pilot and co-pilot – routines must be worked out, and there must be a full understanding of commands between the two and a rehearsal of emergency situations.

One further system to improve the safety aspect of such a large model is to divide, as far as reasonably possible, the principal flying controls between two or more receivers, although operated from the same transmitter. By having the port aileron, port rudder (for a twin-rudder aeroplane) and port-side elevator operated from one receiver, and the starboard control surfaces working from a second, there is every chance, should one receiver fail, that the model will still have sufficient control to bring it back and land it safely. Of course, other safety features such as battery-backers for receivers and separate batteries for servos, plus fail-safe systems on all receivers, are included.

Even when dual or triple receiver installations are not incorporated, it is still possible to use servos in such a way that a degree of duplication is included as a safeguard in the event of a servo failure. By having separate servos operating the ailerons and elevator halves there should be sufficient control from one servo to fly the model should the other fail. The only time that this would not be so is if the servo failed when it was at full, or near full, deflection. An alternative to having separate servos for, say, the elevator is to 'twin' the servos, connect them with a linking bar and have the take-off for the pushrod linkage from the bar. In this case, if one servo does fail there would still be 50 per cent of the total movement available from the remaining servo.

## Fail-safe

Having spoken previously about fail-safe systems, and the limitations of these devices, it is good to know that there are developments coming along that should further improve safety. Interference to the radio signal, often from one of our own R/C operators through bad discipline, is the chief cause of R/C-initiated crashes. That is a bold statement and one that may be challenged by modellers who prefer to lay the blame at the feet of the manufacturers. However, from personal experience over many years, I believe that the signal from another transmitter on the same frequency causes more crashes than equipment failure. As we have seen, when this happens at present, the receiver (or probably both of them if the 'interfering' outfit is also switched on) locks out and a sequence of events takes place to position the servos.

Incidentally, in military drones this is often accompanied by a solenoid-released parachute to return the aircraft to earth, even in the event of total battery failure. Unfortunately, it is not practical to fit parachutes to all our models; there is insufficient space in many of them, and attempting to fit a parachute large enough to bring the model down at a sensible rate of descent, for a scale biplane or many other types, is impossible.

Ideally, if interference is received on one frequency the transmitter and receiver should be capable of automatically switching to a reserve frequency. I state automatically because I have seen models with back-up transmitters and receivers where the theory is that if one system fails, the transmitter is switched off and instructions given to the operator of the standby transmitter to switch

on and continue to fly the model. In practice what happens is that the pilot suspects that there is something amiss with the model, but he is initially uncertain whether it is, perhaps, wind disturbance, or even pilot-induced problems. By the time he is convinced that it is indeed a radio failure, has the wit to switch off his transmitter and give the command to his standby pilot, it is all too late – and the model crashes. It does not take long for a model, with total radio failure, to descend from a height of 100 metres, and you would have to be very quick 'on the button' to pass over the control and save the aircraft. On the two occasions I have witnessed this occurrence the result has been crashes.

There are now in pre-production stages transmitter/receiver combinations where there is an automatic switch-over from the main transmitter frequency to the reserve frequency. This basically involves having two transmitter circuits with both transmitter frequencies operative, but the

*Operating a dual-frequency transmitter – note the twin aerials.*

receiver only switches over in the event of the loss of an acceptable signal on the primary frequency. There are difficulties in having both the primary and standby frequencies from the same frequency band width, for example 35MHz or, for surface vehicles, 40MHz; these problems arise from both technical and practical reasons, the latter being that it would 'tie up' two 'spot' frequencies every time a modeller operated one of these dual-frequency systems. There is also the possibility of the interference being completely across the board, ie blanket interference through the spectrum of that frequency band; this does not happen very often, but once is enough.

What is needed for this system to be truly practical is an allocation of a 'safety band' frequency that is used only for the back-up transmissions. We are not looking to use these frequencies as an alternative operating frequency, just for the time it takes to appreciate that there is a problem on the primary transmission and to land the model safely. There is the 27MHz band, but as this is used by all and sundry it is hardly a safe band to switch on to in the event of a primary failure. I am not advocating that all models should use the dual-frequency system, but it is an extra safety device that would be particularly sensible to introduce for very large scale models. These are the types that would be displayed at public events and this is where there are likely to be R/C model cars and boats being demonstrated, some using the 27MHz frequency.

It is to be hoped that the radio regulatory authorities will see the wisdom of introducing such an additional safety feature and allocate a small width waveband for this purpose.

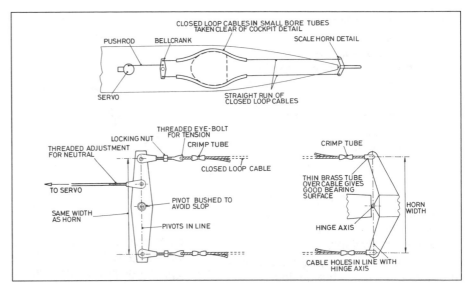

*Closed-loop linkage systems offer light, positive control with low weight and inertia. For larger models a bellcrank is required, either at the servo or the control surface end. This large P-47 'Thunderbolt' model has a 240 cc flat four engine.*

## Linkages

Although the linkages to the control surfaces and other controls are not part and parcel of the radio equipment, it is important to understand the types used and their functions, as they do indirectly affect the equipment.

A poorly installed linkage, for instance, can put undue strain on the servo. Also, you may have no transmitter function for differential control or mixing, and this will have to be arranged mechanically. It is, in any case, important to know as much as possible about the equipment, installation and alternative means of making adjustments, as it will provide more options and allow you to take the best available action.

Using the electronic adjustments available on the transmitter is not always the best method, even if it is the easiest. Any model – aeroplane, car, boat or helicopter – has to be trimmed out to perform well. This can be done mechanically, by adjusting clevises, control throws, pushrods, etc, or it can, in most cases, be achieved electronically. For non-computer sets, where fine trimming relies on the mechanical/electrical trim levers on the transmitter, it is important to use these for initial trimming only. For instance, a boat may be turning consistently to port when the control stick is centralised, so the trim lever is moved to the right to correct the turn. When the sailing of the boat is completed the linkage between the servo and the rudder should be adjusted so that the rudder is in the revised position with the control stick centralised. The trim lever can also then be centralised. This is good practice even with computerised sets; it may be that, by using the electronic trim movement, the overall range of servo movement you should have is minimised.

Planning your linkage route is most important, as we want to get from the servo to the control surface as directly as possible. Linkages, to be effective, need to be as friction-free as possible, have no wasted movement and to

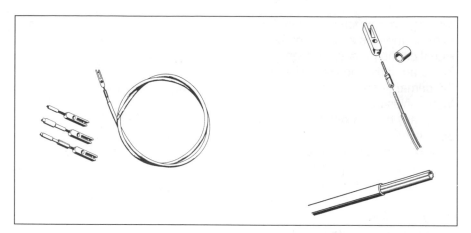

'Snake', or 'tube and cable', linkages can be in the form of metal cable in tube (the Bowden cable familiar on bicycles), nylon rod in tube (as in the second drawing), or tube in tube (as in the third). Appropriate end fittings are available.

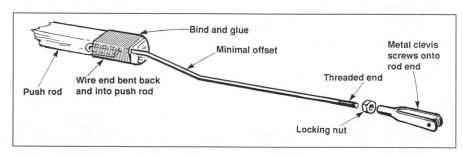

Pushrods should have threaded rod ends as short as possible and with minimum offsets. For larger models the pushrod should be from glass fibre or aluminium tubing.

have minimum inertia (in a crash, a heavy pushrod can easily damage the servo output gears through the inertial effects). As often happens in life, we seem to have to re-invent systems and methods to get the best results.

In the early days of R/C flying, closed-loop control systems were widely used and were effective. However, as more and more accessories became available, for example moulded horns, clevises, adaptors, etc, the pushrod linkage system became popular and the closed loop systems all but disappeared. When considered logically, closed-loop control has much to recommend it. It is very lightweight, very positive (always acting in the 'pull' mode) and frictionless. Three out of three –

not bad! The disadvantages are that it is not always possible, or convenient, to have direct routes from the servo to the control horns, but this can be overcome by taking the control runs through narrow-bore tubing, but some of the simplicity and effectiveness is lost.

One other potential disadvantage with a closed-loop system is the strain it can place on the servo output, with the closed-loop cables pulling on the output arm. With moderate-sized models and ballraced servo outputs this is not a problem, although the control cables should not be over-tightened. For larger models it is wise to incorporate a bellcrank between the servo and the control surface so that the servo operates the bellcrank with a short pushrod.

It may also be that it is inconvenient to take the closed loop control all the way to the control surface, for example an elevator, and here again a 180-degree bellcrank can be inserted and the final connection to the control horn made by a short adjustable pushrod.

Pushrods from the servo to the control surface horn need to be rigid but light – flexing will cause inaccuracies in the control. Wire-threaded rod ends, usually bicycle spokes, should be kept reasonably short and without acute bends, again to minimise flexing. For larger models glass fibre rods, such as fishing rod sections, can be usefully employed, while for smaller models carbon fibre archery arrow shafts are both light and extremely rigid. Alternatives to these materials are traditional balsa wood, a good cross-section, straight-grain selection; for small and medium-sized models only, because it is 'whippy', beech dowel may be used.

Many are the materials and sections used in the so-called control 'snakes'. These consist of an inner core (the pushrod or cable of the linkage) and an outer tube to restrain the inner. Most modellers will be familiar with the Bowden cable systems used on bicycles, and 'snake' linkages work on the same principles. Indeed, Bowden cable, with a nylon tube outer and multi-core steel cable inner, is used for R/C modelling purposes. Other materials used include solid nylon rod inners, serrated-edged plastic tube inners and straightforward tube-in-tube systems, all using one of the modern man-made plastics.

Adaptors are available for all of these systems so that adjustable connectors can be attached to the servo and control horn ends. The outer cables must be adequately supported throughout their run, the ends have to be properly secured so that there is no fore and aft movement, and sufficient distance must be left between the outer and inner materials to give full linkage movement. However, inners and adaptors too inadequately supported by the outer tubing, will again lead to unwanted flexing. Curves can be formed in the 'snakes', but these should not be of too small a radius otherwise there will be excessive lost movement, and they will also introduce more friction.

Bellcranks are basically used for changes of direction of linkage through 90 degrees, 180 degrees or any angle in between. Although this is their main purpose, it is also possible to take advantage of this change of direction to introduce an increase or decrease of movement, or some differential movement.

Differential movement geometry is not the easiest to understand, but it can be introduced at the servo output and by locating the control horn in relation to the control surface hinge. Once the principle is grasped it becomes easy, but it is important, if the differential control is to be mechanical, to consider it carefully at the planning stage. Go back to first principles and check that your proposed geometry of servo outputs, bellcranks or control horn locations is giving you the differential movement in the direction required. Perhaps it is not surprising that modellers opt for 'dialling in' the required differential electronically when this is available on the transmitter.

## Mechanical mixing

In the chapter dealing with computerised R/C equipment we saw how the mixing of various controls, for example elevator/flaps, or rudder/aileron, can be programmed into the transmitter. It is also possible to arrange for mixing controls, including 'elevons' and 'V' tail

*Mechanical mixers, for 'ruddervators' or 'flaperons', are commercially available or can be simply constructed with piano wire rods and a servo with sliding tubes.*

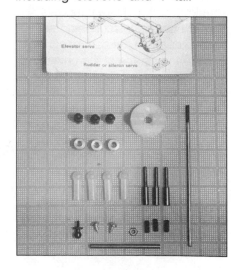

arrangements, by mechanical means. What is not possible, in the case of mixing elevator and flaps, or rudder and aileron, is to un-couple these during flight. Whether the coupling is by mechanical means only, ie pushrods and cranks from one servo, or whether two servos are operated via a 'Y' lead from one receiver output, the coupling is constant until it is physically disconnected.

## Strong, secure, smooth and 'slop' free

Before closing this chapter it is worth re-emphasising the need for a well-considered and well-executed control linkage system. It must be strong – you can always test it by giving a good strong pull at the points where you would expect to get the maximum loads; it must be secure – with none of the clevises too near to the end of the threaded rod and bellcranks securely fixed; and the operation must be smooth – if the linkage from the servo is disconnected and operated over the full range of movement there should be no excess free play in the linkage system, holes where clevises and rods are attached should not be oversize, pushrods should not be flexing and cranks should not be rocking. If there is play at one end, disconnect the linkage or move the control surface to trace the source of the unwanted movement and eliminate it. There are few more frightening occurrences than watching a model aeroplane suffering from aileron or elevator flutter, almost invariably caused by poor linkages and hinging allowing unwanted free movement up and down.

No mention here is made of control surface hinges – that must be a subject for the model-making publications.

*When there are such magnificent radio control models at stake, it pays to ensure that the radio systems, linkages and hinges are all in perfect order.*

# Chapter 5

# Model boats

Under this general heading we will be considering R/C equipment and installations of boats, ships and yachts.

## Which mode?

The equipment used for boats is essentially similar to that operated in model aeroplanes and helicopters, as previously described, although it is seldom that as many functions are required by the boat modellers. Simple boats are operated by two-function R/C outfits, one channel for steering (rudder) and one for engine control (throttle for internal combustion (IC) engines, speed controller for electrics). The transmitter for the two-function can comprise a single, double-axis stick, or, more likely, twin single-axis sticks. In the latter case the standard arrangement is for steering to be on the right of the transmitter, operating horizontally, and the motor control on the left, operating vertically with the high position as full power.

When more than two functions are used, the same 'Mode' decisions need to be made as those that face the model aircraft flyers. In this case it would be whether to have both of the two primary controls (rudder and throttle) on the right-hand stick, or separate them between the two sticks, and which to have on each. There appear to be more 'split stick' operators in the boating world than in flying. In common

*A typical low-cost two-function radio outfit suited to non-competition sports boats.*

with flying, the rudder control is self-centring (the transmitter stick is spring-loaded) and the throttle is progressive, ie the servo stays at the last stick command, the stick being friction-held by a ratchet system. All transmitter mechanical/electrical trims, ie the trim levers, are non-centring.

## Servos

Servos, too, are similar to the products previously described, but because the boats are operating in the unfriendly environment of water, water-resistant types should be used. These were at one time referred to as waterproof servos, but to my knowledge few of them were genuinely waterproof, and water has a nasty habit of forcing its way into the most minute of

holes and cracks. Occasionally a boat is going to become submerged, and it is not good enough to assume that the water-resistant servo will cope in this situation – and I mean survive, not operate. Additional waterproofing arrangements will have to be made.

## Sails

One variation on the servo theme comes with the operation of yachts. Here we need to pull in the sails or let them out so that they are at the most efficient angles to the wind. For this we have to pull on sheets (ropes to the non-sailor, or, in modelling terms, cord), and a simple 90 degree movement of a servo output is insufficient. Following full-size practice, the

Many racing boats, including twin-hulled designs, turn virtually 'flat'. With a greater risk of models flipping onto their backs there is a real need for careful water-proofing. Note the sealed panels and the 'bellows' cover to the rudder linkage.

Sail winch servos can be supplied with extended servo arms or winch drums; sometimes there are drums of different diameters on each side of the servo for small and large sails, and good torque characteristics are required. The servo illustrated with the alternative drum sizes is the same 'Mammoth' servo previously illustrated in kit form.

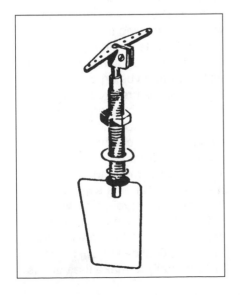

considerable, and for this reason the winch is geared down and strong metal gears are fitted. However, the gearing cannot be too great, otherwise operational speed will be lost and, in racing, this is not acceptable. The only sensible answer is to use a powerful motor and to provide it with a separate power supply. Whereas the normal servo output moves on either side of neutral by 40 degrees or so, the sail winch rotates through a number of turns and is non-centring. It might be thought of as the 'power' control.

## Steering

Steering, if we exclude specialist water pumping and swivelling power systems, is by the rudder (boats have no equivalent to an aileron, and will take up a bank angle naturally when this is needed and as speed dictates – some designs, such as twin hulls, turn virtually 'flat').

For many of the non-speed-competitive boats the load on the rudder is relatively small, but larger designs and the high-speed types put a greater load on the servo. In these instances it is prudent to use a balanced rudder, with the hinge point giving about ⅛th of the rudder area in front and ⅞ths behind. A suitable output servo is then selected for control.

## Engine speed control

For IC (ie glow and diesel) engined boats the control is as before; a servo is linked to the throttle arm of the carburettor so that full power is obtained when the throttle stick on the transmitter is pushed fully up, with the trim lever also fully up. With the stick fully down, the engine should be at a safe idle, and when the trim lever is also pulled down, the engine should stop.

*A commercial brass rudder and horn linkage. This is a balanced rudder with the hinge point behind the leading edge.*

sheet is rotated around a winch drum and the yacht servo therefore has drums installed axially one above another or on each side of the servo for the jib and main sail. The drum diameters may vary to give different winding speeds for the sails.

With larger yachts the power required to haul the sails in against the pressure of the wind is very

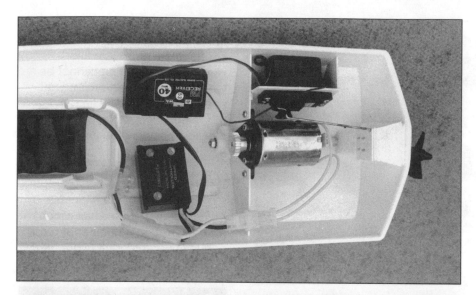

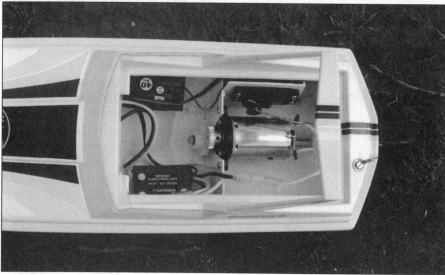

*The layout of the radio equipment should be checked before final installation – this is a two-channel outfit for rudder and speed-controller operation. A hatch will provide a degree of waterproofing.*

Electric motors are, naturally, a popular power form for boats of all types, but particularly scale types where the sound of an IC engine contributes nothing towards the impression of reality. For controlling the electric motor the standard speed controllers are recommended, size only becoming important with the fast electric boats; these have none too much space for radio and battery installations and the boaters want to cram into that space as much

potential power as possible. Hence the requirement for physically small electronic speed controllers, but which are capable of coping with large amperages. Fortunately, the boat modellers have gained in this respect from the car racing fraternity, where there were similar requirements, and the manufacturers have come up with the goods.

At the simplest level it is possible to use micro-switches, operated from a cam device cut in the servo output disc, to switch the

current on and off. If a bank of these switches is fitted around the servo and the cam wheel cut accordingly (this is where the large-output discs come in handy) a series of speeds, forward and reverse, can be obtained. Again, there is usually more than one way of achieving an end result, mechanically or electrically.

## Special effects

Auxiliary controls are most likely to be used in scale models where authentic effects are aimed for, to represent the prototype boat or ship. For military types the controls may include the operation of the gun turrets, firing of the guns, deployment of depth charges and firing of torpedoes, which feasibly could be radio-controlled also. Merchant and fishing boats could have facilities to drop anchor, lower lifeboats, cast out and haul in fishing nets, etc. All of the boats, for extra effect, could be fitted with radar scanners and lights.

Unlike aircraft, where a range of events do not follow in sequence (with the possible exception of retracting undercarriages), the systems on boats can be sequenced, and do not have to be carried out at high speeds. There are a number of ways of achieving this series of events (turrets turning, guns firing, fire breaking out, sirens sounding, water cannons being operated, etc). It can be pre-programmed, and there are commercially available units for such display events, or they can be controlled individually from the transmitter. This does not mean that each operation requires a separate function and servo – a servo output can be linked to a rotary or semi-rotary switching device and the knob, or slide switch, moved incrementally to make the various

A much greater air of realism will be added to the military vessels if firing guns, smoke generation and noise simulation are added. Commercial units are available for producing all types of noises associated with ships, for example sirens, hooters and whistles, or you can make such items as flasher units yourself, seen here in close-up from both sides.

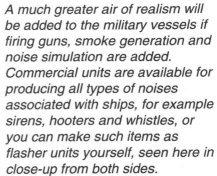

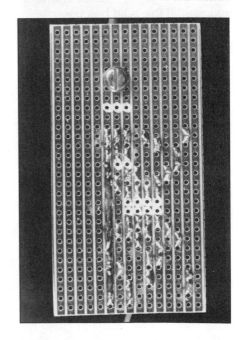

contacts. In this manner four or five functions can be operated from the one progressive control.

One of the most interesting innovations for electric-powered boats in recent years is the use of simulated engine and other sounds. Boat modellers have an advantage at present over car and aviation enthusiasts by having sound to accompany movement – and, for steam-powered models, authentic smells. By linking the electronic sound generator to the speed controller it is also possible to give the impression of correct engine speeds. Add to this the sound of sirens and horns and it provides a new scale dimension.

## Waterproof installation

Consider the worst – it may happen. Water is a very unfriendly element for radio, even more so when it is salt water. Get your radio equipment soaking wet and you have got real problems. With 'good' water you may be able to dry off the equipment by the application of a hair dryer to the exterior of servos, batteries and switches, and the interior of the receiver. If the boat has been immersed in salt water for any period of time your problems are much greater. In this condition the components must be first cleaned with tap water, then dried slowly with a hair dryer and inspected, very carefully, for any corrosion. It is the one time where I would suggest dismantling the servo, just to check that no salt water has entered the interior. If it has, and it is a standard, inexpensive servo, then 'chuck it' and buy a new one. For an expensive servo, do not try to repair it yourself, but send it to the servicing agent with an honest note of what happened. However, the best answer is not to let it happen in the first place.

*The most difficult of all marine craft to waterproof are undoubtedly submarines, where standards have to be 100 per cent. Note the bolt-down clear plastic covers to the radio compartments, the purpose-designed waterproof module and the bellows protection to the linkages.*

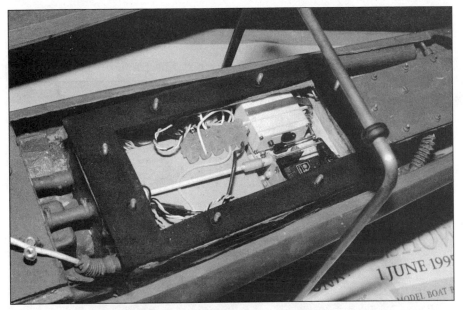

*Earlier designs of servos had linear outputs (sometimes combined rotary and linear outputs), and these are particularly suitable for boats where the servos are close to the wall of the waterproof compartment.*

How you waterproof the radio equipment in the boat will depend on the type and size of the model. For fast electric and some other racing boats and hydrofoils there will not be sufficient space to have separate waterproof radio boxes, but waterproofing is even more essential with these types. With the speed and risk of contact with other boats, markers and other obstacles, there is every chance that the boats will get very wet indeed.

Where a separate box is not possible, a compartment in the boat, usually at the rear, must be waterproofed, with particular attention being paid to the hatch. If the hatch is made from a transparent material it is possible to inspect the installation of the radio equipment without having to break the hatch seal. For absolute waterproofing, for models that may be tipped or inverted for example, a screw-down hatch is essential, with a rigid clear top cover. With the compartment, including any wood linings, treated with an epoxy or similar GRP resin, the top surface, which supports the removable hatch, should be as level and smooth as possible. Self-tapping screws are suitable for fixing the hatches of most boats, but if the hatch is likely to require frequent removal, the use of insert nuts (as used for moulding into plastic) or other forms of captive nuts is recommended. These, with the use of bolts and an electric screwdriver, will allow the hatch to be removed more rapidly, a very desirable feature when water can be seen on the inside of the radio compartment – it can cause panic!

Simply screwing the clear sheet to the plastic or timber is not sufficient; to obtain a watertight seal it will need some resilient material between the two surfaces. Self-adhesive (one side) waterproof silicone tape about 2 mm thick can be purchased from such suppliers as Cirkit and Radio Spares, and this will form a 'bed' for the hatch; sealant can then be stuck to the boat and the top screwed down. Where the sealant is going to touch the plastic, a smear of petroleum jelly is used to prevent the hatch from sticking to the sealant. Even with this silicone bed the joint should be treated with a thin film of silicone grease when the hatch is tightened, and a little also applied to the fixing screws.

Unfortunately, our lovely watertight box has to be pierced with holes to allow the pushrods to reach steering arms, carburettors, etc, as well as allowing for the aerial lead. For the latter, a rubber grommet with a small hole, of similar size to the aerial, and some silicone sealant (lightly grease the aerial when first fitting) should give a water-resistant result; that is, it will be OK provided that the boat is not fully submerged.

For the pushrods the problems occur when the output of the servo is close to the exit point of the box, so that the rotary motion of the output is still apparent at the exit location. A flexible outlet may be used, either a commercial bellows type or the neck of a child's balloon. To reduce the rotary element it might be possible to jury rig the linkage, ie to take it initially in the opposite direction before doubling back and exiting the compartment. This may be suitable for linkages to the engine throttle, but would not be sufficiently direct and free from play for a rudder linkage on a powerful boat.

With control linkage 'snakes' the outer cable is glued to the compartment exit with epoxy (or one of the many modern adhesives now designed to glue 'greasy' plastics) – but you should check that there is no binding being caused by the distance between the servo and the compartment wall. There is a definite case, here, for the return of the linear servo, or the fitting of rotary-to-linear-output adaptors.

Small model boats, such as those that were not originally intended for R/C operation, can now be converted to remote control thanks to the miniaturisation of equipment, but give different waterproofing problems. There is not room in most of them for separate compartments or separate R/C equipment boxes; all that is possible is to protect the more vulnerable items individually.

The receiver can be wrapped in a plastic bag, the top sealed and a small silica gel bag (containing hydroscopic crystals) put in with the receiver to prevent condensation. The same treatment can be given to the battery and switch (allowing access to the charging socket), but little can be done to protect the servos. Small boats of this type are not likely to be sailed in anything but indoor pools, so there is much less likelihood of them getting a real soaking.

## 'Lunchbox' waterproofing

Some of the superior polythene lunch boxes have excellent airtight – and waterproof – lids. Indeed, the smaller round Tupperware containers have been used for fuel tanks before now and have served well in that role. When you are less than sure about the effectiveness of the lid seal it can always be further reinforced with the application of freezer tape over the seal. The idea, of course, is to fit all of your radio equipment in the box, then secure the box into the hull of the boat. Purpose-made boxes are available from your model shop in a variety of sizes and with certain fittings for switches, charging sockets, etc.

The majority of R/C boats will use the 'radio in a box' system of

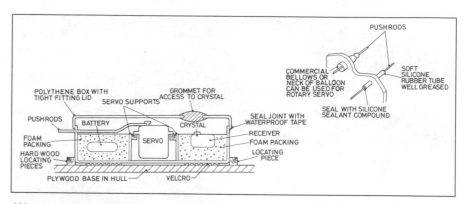

*Waterproofing of boats can be achieved by mounting the radio equipment in a plastic food container, then positioning this in the hull of the boat.*

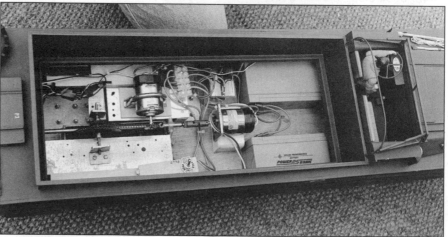

*This excellent model of an amphibian 'Duck' is only intended for 'calm weather' boating-pool operation. Waterproofing may not be complete and any water ingress would have to be dealt with immediately.*

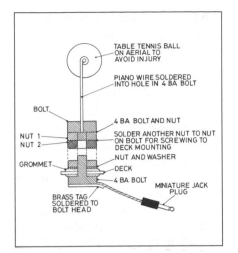

*A commercial aerial has the advantage of being easily dismantled for transport, although the home-made aerial can be similarly adapted for removal.*

*When sailing boats with the operators in close proximity to one another, it is sensible to protect the ends of the transmitter aerial, perhaps with a plastic practice golf ball.*

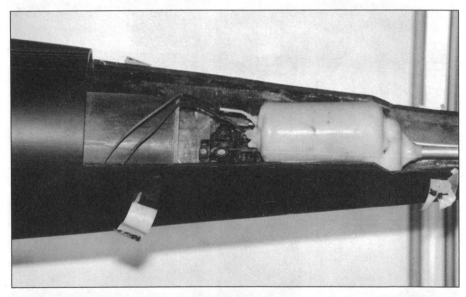

*One to prove the exception to the rule, this submarine has a 'potted' electric motor but servos that are regularly subjected to full immersion. No problems have been experienced with the 'waterproof' servos.*

installation, which has obvious advantages with regard to waterproofing, but also has a few limitations. Fitting wooden servo rails to the plastic box is not easy; use a glue that is truly compatible with the material (do a test run on some scrap). Also the bogey of servo linkages being close to the exit point may occur, so go for as large a box as will conveniently fit into the boat and be careful to pre-plan the installation.

With the box being removable – although in some cases it could be permanently fixed to the boat – it is more difficult to keep the linkages positive. Every effort has to be made to ensure that the box fits into exactly the same position each time and that, being flexible, it is not going to move around. By using locating rails, side restraints and substantial retaining rubber bands this is not too difficult, and the repeatable accuracy is certainly more than adequate for sport and scale boats. Moulded GRP and vacformed hulls provide a little more of a challenge in making a 'repeatable position'

location for the box, and in these cases the angles of the recess can be built up with a resin to 'cup' the corners of the box each time it is inserted.

Naturally it is best to avoid removing the box wherever

possible, or even the lid. Holes can be cut in the lid over specific areas, for example the switch, charging socket and servo outputs, and blind grommets (the sort you will find in the floor of the boot of your car – to let water out!) fitted in

*Electronics extravaganza! This submarine, built and fitted out by John Robinson, will not only carry out all the functions of the prototype but it is also fitted with a video camera for sending back pictures as it submerges. Absolute waterproofing is certainly a must for this highly complex installation – just look at the wiring looms!*

the holes. They must, however, be a good fit and the grommets carefully replaced.

When water accidentally enters a boat for whatever reason, it is going to finish up in the bottom of the hull – unless the boat has been tipped upside down. It should therefore be obvious that the higher the equipment is mounted in the hull, the less likely it is to get wet, and unless balance reasons to maintain a low centre of gravity dictate otherwise, this principle should be followed. The actual waterproof box does not automatically have to be raised above the floor of the hull; if a tall box is used the equipment can be mounted high.

Yachts offer rather different problems as the weight distribution is very much concentrated around the lower part of the keel and any additional weight above this level is going to be to the detriment of sailing efficiency. One of the heaviest components of the R/C equipment in the boat is the batteries, one for the receiver and probably a separate one for the winch servo. For maximum performance, at the expense of risk, the nicad packs can be positioned in the bulb keel. 'Potting' the batteries in GRP resin is not to be recommended as the nicad cells are of the vented types, but it is possible to make substantial GRP moulded housings and bolt on hatches so that access, in the event of a failure, is possible. Remember that a yacht is going to be sailing with its deck awash for much of the time, which calls for even more care with the waterproofing of hatches and the winch in particular.

Racing can result in the need to change frequency crystals on a fairly regular basis, and it is not easy to make special provision for this. It should be possible for the

*Whether you want to haul in your catch, paddle your own canoe, or just iron out the waves (overleaf), all is possible with radio equipment and a passion!*

manufacturers to devise a crystal holder extension so that this can be placed in a separate, more easily accessible, container.

Aerials may be of the standard type, as fitted to the receiver, or in whip aerial form. Commercial whip aerials are available, or they are easily made from piano wire – always remember to put a small loop, or bead, at the top of the aerial to allow it to be more easily seen and prevent injury to someone's eye. The whip aerial is usually removable by unscrewing at deck, or radio box, level, and may also have a plug and socket close to the receiver. Whether it has one or two connectors, the overall length should be the same as the original aerial length from the receiver case to the tip of the aerial.

Many modellers have serious doubts about the R/C operation of submarines when they are

swimming bath operation, where the water is clear and the craft can be observed. Most important with the submarine, of course, is the absolute waterproofing of all hatches, and double seals may be needed in these circumstances.

Other general matters regarding installation and operation can be found in the preceding chapters.

## Inspection

Regular inspection of the R/C equipment is a must for model boats – check, check and check again for contamination by water. If you catch it early it will probably not have done any damage, but always clean the components thoroughly and give a final spray with an electrical component cleaner (available from one of the major component suppliers).

submerged. There is no need to worry, for the signals are still received and the range is more than adequate for any normal purpose. I cannot imagine the model

submariner taking his boat out into the sea or a river, putting her below and motoring off into the vast dark unknown. Submarines would seem to be more suited to, typically,

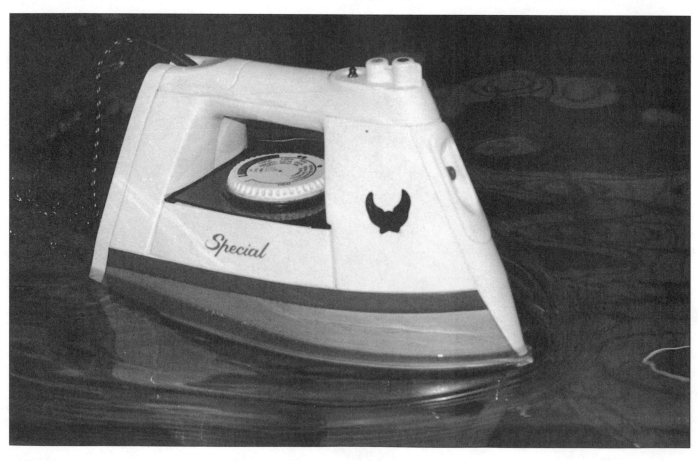

# Chapter 6

# Cars

The variety of R/C cars is now very considerable and still growing. They range from the small, inexpensive, ready-to-go toy, with basic steering and speed control, to the increasingly large R/C off-road cars. There are track racing cars, stock cars, off-road racers, buggies, go-carts, scale cars and trucks. Most have electric motor power, but IC engines are still used for quite a few of the racing classes, and spark ignition engines (converted from chainsaw engines) are now being used in some of the larger off-road racers.

## Transmitters and receivers

Radio control equipment for cars is not vastly different from that used in aircraft or boats, except in one respect. Transmitters may be of the same format as the two-stick types and these can have programmes (for computer sets) with special car functions and features, but there is no direct comparison between the operation of a full-size car and the model car when using a 'standard' transmitter; one uses a steering wheel while the other uses levers being moved sideways.

Perhaps for this reason the radio manufacturers introduced a new style of transmitter for operating land vehicles, substituting a wheel for the stick, the throttle being operated by a pistol grip. Two-channel equipment

*A small selection from the very wide range of cars and trucks available. Costs of the kits and the radio equipment can also vary from a few pounds to many hundreds.*

is adequate for sports class cars, where the lower half of the throttle quadrant is used for braking control, but three channel-equipment is becoming increasingly popular.

The serious racing enthusiast would certainly not consider anything less than a three-function (channel) outfit, and this would probably be a PCM computer type. With a number of cars operating close to one another and with the drivers standing cheek by jowl on the drivers' rostrum, it is essential that the equipment has close frequency control and that the receiver has excellent adjacent channel interference rejection. Where FM radio is used in racing, it would be advisable to have a dual conversion receiver.

Purpose-designed receivers for car operation are smaller and lighter than the aircraft types and the latest use surface-mounting technology for better damage resistance. The transmitter will have all the basic functions of the other computer systems, for example rates, 'end point' adjustment, exponential, etc, but will also have specific functions for cars:

Rotary control brake travel adjustment
Rotary control steering travel adjustment
Independent throttle and brake travel adjustment
Variable steering trim rate
Steering balance adjustment
Two steering curves – exponential
Two independent throttle/brake curves – exponential
Throttle pre-set button for instant full power or motor stop
Trim off-set warning, indicating any accidental trim movement between sessions
Elapsed timer or countdown timer
Lap timer with individual lap memory

*Steering-wheel-type transmitters, with a trigger-operated throttle, are favoured by some modellers; popularity will also vary from country to country.*

The transmitter programme will have a model memory, typically six cars, it will have PCM and PPM modulation options, the PCM with a fail-safe facility, and DSC (Direct Servo Control). The latter function is particularly important for car racing where a great deal of servicing is carried out between heats or races. Servo adjustments may be part of the modifications and without DSC any changes would involve a lot of guesswork.

Whether the operator prefers the standard, stick-operated transmitter or the pistol-grip style with a miniature steering wheel is entirely an open option and not one that it is possible to advise upon. Before purchasing it would be worthwhile checking out the two varieties – your local car club could probably arrange this.

## Servo savers

Racing cars, and off-road buggies even more so, lead a pretty tough life. The racing environment might not be quite as horrendous as salt water, but it is still pretty grim. Wet grass, sand, rocks and pools have to be traversed and the rough terrain means that the car is receiving a lot of bumps and shocks. If all these shock loads were transferred direct from the steering linkage to the servo, the latter's life would be very short. To reduce the risk of damage to the output, which is normally ballraced in racing car servos, and the gear train, a 'servo saver' is fitted. This spring-loaded device takes out the worst of the shock loads without adversely effecting the steering accuracy.

A system of over-ride springs is used on the throttle servo when it is also used for braking. From a neutral position the throttle opens normally as it is advanced, but when the throttle lever is pulled back the throttle spring is compressed (as the throttle reaches its minimum idle speed setting) and operates the brake – which also has a spring-loaded over-ride when the opposite movement takes place.

## Installation

Except for a few hand-made military vehicles, tanks, landing craft, etc, nearly all model land vehicles are constructed from kits, or are 'almost ready to drive'. Full instructions will be given regarding the placement of the radio equipment, the linkages, batteries and motors. This applies whether the vehicle is a 'Funny car', a

*Not a steering wheel or pistol grip in sight! These drivers all prefer the standard, two-stick transmitters. Serious racing enthusiasts will operate the latest computerised PCM radio equipment, with the programming and adjustments offered by these systems.*

'Servo savers', or over-rides, can be of the spring return type (as seen in the first group of drawings), ideal for the throttle and brake operation where adjustments can be rapidly made, or the 'knock-away' units, which may be preferred for steering linkages. Most car kits will have these items included as part of the contents.

scale commercial vehicle or a ⅛th scale IC-powered full racing car. If you do not have the exact radio equipment specified for the model you may have to make minor modifications but, in general, keep to the instructions and you should have few problems.

For 'scratch-built' vehicles use the standard installation techniques previously mentioned in this book, selecting servos and batteries to match the project and taking into consideration whether the equipment will have a gentle life, for example a model road transporter, or have to put up with rugged conditions, such as a replica JCB earth-mover.

Model car kits are generally very well engineered and

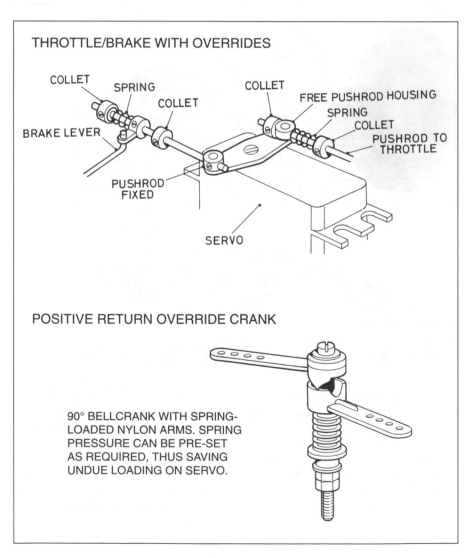

THROTTLE/BRAKE WITH OVERRIDES

POSITIVE RETURN OVERRIDE CRANK

90° BELLCRANK WITH SPRING-LOADED NYLON ARMS. SPRING PRESSURE CAN BE PRE-SET AS REQUIRED, THUS SAVING UNDUE LOADING ON SERVO.

*Loads on servos can be high with IC-powered off-road racers, so suitable power servos must be used, with rugged output arms, linkages and over-ride systems.*

comprehensive, the electric-powered models being supplied with the motors, while some, of the basic two-function type, may also be supplied complete with radio equipment. Being designed with care and to close limits, there is not much wasted space in R/C cars, and the radio installation is all planned for you. Servo locations are moulded into the chassis components, so you may have to use a particular size of servo (there is not too much difference in the size of comparable servos from various manufacturers). Linkages will also be supplied, and the illustrated instructions leave little danger of not knowing where the various components fit.

There may be a protective radio 'box' with the kit – it very

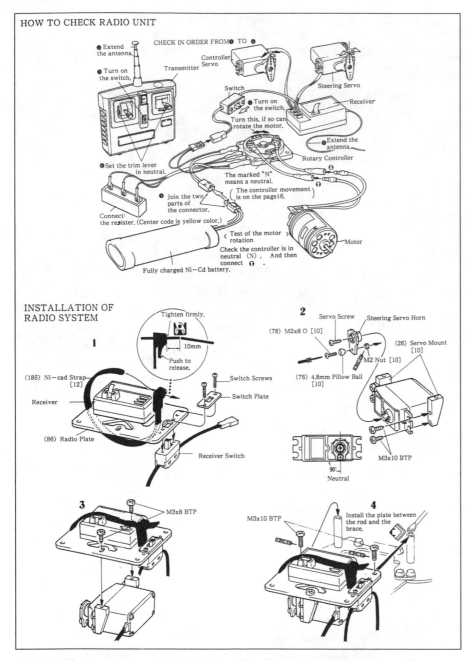

HOW TO CHECK RADIO UNIT

CHECK IN ORDER FROM ❶ TO ❼

- Extend the antenna.
- Turn on the switch.
- Set the trim lever in neutral.

Transmitter

Controller Servo

Switch
- Turn on the switch.

Turn this, if so can rotate the motor.

Steering Servo

Receiver

- Extend the antenna.

Rotary Controller

The marked "N" means a neutral.
( The controller movement is on the page16. )

- Join the two parts of the connector.

Connect the resister. (Center code is yellow color.)

Test of the motor rotation
Check the controller is in neutral (N). And then connect ❼.

Motor

Fully charged Ni−Cd battery.

INSTALLATION OF RADIO SYSTEM

**1**

Tighten firmly.

10mm

Push to release.

(185) Ni−cad Strap [12]

Receiver

(86) Radio Plate

Switch Screws

Switch Plate

Receiver Switch

**2**

Servo Screw    Steering Servo Horn

(78) M2x8 O [10]

(26) Servo Mount [10]

M2 Nut [10]

(76) 4.8mm Pillow Ball [10]

M3x10 BTP

90°
Neutral

**3**

M3x8 BTP

**4**

M3x10 BTP

Install the plate between the rod and the brace.

*Pictorial instructions are included in all radio car assembly kits – all you have to do is to be sure of following the methods and sequences. The Kyosho instructions shown here are typical of those to be found in popular, inexpensive car kits.*

much depends on the model design – but this will not be watertight as with the boat versions mentioned in the last chapter. The box will, however, keep the worst of the splashes, mud and general dross from the radio. If the radio is basically unprotected, some vehicles of the racing class specification make it impossible to fit such luxuries, so you must keep a close watch on all the electrics and electronics on the car; at least the receiver should be protected in a plastic bag.

## Speed control

Although resistor-type controllers for electric cars were popular a few years ago, operated by a servo moving a contact across an etched printed circuit board, these items were quite bulky and required a high degree of servicing. The advantages of the electronic speed controller are considerable; they can incorporate reverse and braking facilities and BEC (battery eliminator circuitry).

Allied to the small overall size and weight, the electronic speed controller is suitable for a wide range of electric-powered vehicles, including the smallest, where the lack of the receiver battery is another blessing. Designed to operate at 7.2 to 8.4 volts, the higher-specification speed controllers will accept a surge current in excess of 500 amps and include thermal overload protection to cut the power if over-heating occurs. When fitting the speed controller it is important to check that connections are being made with the correct polarity – reversed polarity could cause severe damage.

## Care and maintenance

Racing cars, by their nature, require a high degree of maintenance and repair, and the operator is likely to notice anything wrong with the radio equipment.

In most of the other R/C disciplines the operator keeps relatively clean, but with servicing during car racing you are likely to become grubby and sweaty. When you pick up the transmitter after having got the model ready for the next race, your hands are not going to be in the cleanest state, so give the transmitter a clean from time to time, and include in the cleaning the collapsible aerial.

*Simple 'plastic' model car assembly kits and the more sophisticated racing types will have built-in provision for servos, engines and motors, with the linkage systems for steering and power.*

charging and servo output sockets – use switch cleaner (use it on the switch, too) and the receiver aerial. The aerial may well be routed through a vertical tube and be wound back down the outside of the tube, and the range reduction with this arrangement is of little consequence, as the cars are only being operated over short distances (do not try this aerial system with aeroplanes). Check the aerial for any strain on the receiver joint and fraying of the aerial over its full length.

With the heavy loads involved for steering it is normal to use heavier duty servo output arms; if you use standard output arms or discs, check for any cracking or splitting. Security and resilience is required for the receiver and battery installations – not always easy to achieve – and it must be accepted that the car-borne R/C equipment is going to get a considerably tougher life than would be the case in, say, a glider.

This can also get dirty, lose conductivity and have a reduced output range. A clean-up with methylated spirits will help here (as it does with your full-size car aerial!).

Other radio servicing checks include the plugs and sockets – still together and not dirty –

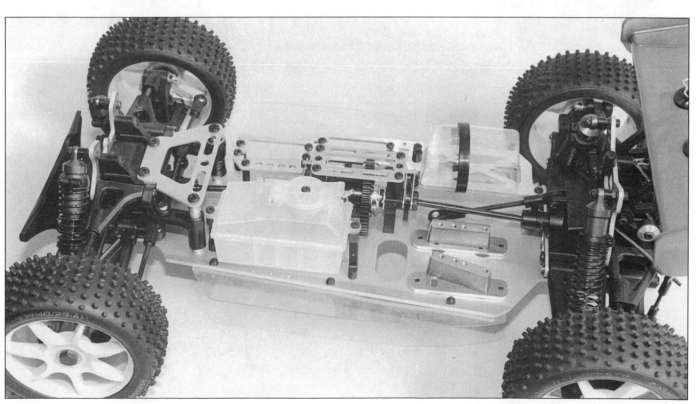

*Variety is the spice of life and there is certainly plenty of variety to be had with vehicles – fast and furious, or slow and sedate.*

# Chapter 7

# Helicopters

When the first R/C helicopter was produced in commercial form in the early 1970s it was a tremendous technical achievement in aerodynamic and mechanical terms. The gearbox arrangements, the rotor head engineering and the drive to the tail rotor all required pioneering work that took years to perfect. Electronic advances in radio control, with proportional control now being available, made the control and flying of the helicopter possible but far from easy, and it was obvious that any advances in control systems that the manufacturers could provide would be more than welcome. It is true to say that the advent of the helicopter and the consequent advancement in its mechanical systems has led to more improvements in radio control than any other development. Fellow R/C disciplines have benefited from these improvements in the standards and capabilities of the radio equipment design, but the demands have come mostly from the helicopter fraternity.

Fixed-pitch helicopters, where ascent and descent is controlled by throttle control, have virtually disappeared from the scene. Although they had the advantages of low cost and only required a four-channel radio outfit, these were outweighed by the difficulties, particularly for the beginner, of mastering hovering flight and the transition to forward flight. Collective pitch is now standard on helicopters, unless specifically

*Radio-controlled helicopters have come a long way since the first faltering flights in 1970. Now they are becoming larger – and more impressive – and are controllable to the extent of being able to be flown from a full-size 'chopper'.*

*Curtis Youngblood, World Champion model helicopter pilot, uses a Mode 3 ('cuddle box') transmitter layout for his 3D-style flying.*

## HELICOPTER TRANSMITTER CONTROLS AND FUNCTIONS

Functions and locations given in this drawing are the factory default positions, which occur upon startup. Each setting can be easily changed as the owner desires. The Function Change menu [FNC] may be used for this purpose.

Handle
7. CH7 Knob/Pitch Trim
5. CH5 Switch (ON in forward position) Rate gyro output switching Inverted switch
17. Normal Flight condition D Idle-up 1 Flight condition 2 Idle-up 2 Flight condition 3 Switch
6. Hovering Pitch Lever
Tachometer Sensor
15. Elevator Dual Rate Switch (ON in lower position)
16. Rudder Dual Rate Switch and CH9
10. Elevator Trim
12. Rudder Trim

CAMPac Memory Module
Antenna
Hovering Throttle Knob
8. CH8 Switch (3 positions)
19. Trainer Switch (ON in forward position)
18. Throttle Hold Switch Flight condition 4
14. Aileron Dual Rate Switch (ON in forward position)
13. Pitch Control High Side Trim Lever
Monitor Lamp
Slantable Stick Adjusting Screw
Power Switch
11. Throttle Trim
9. Aileron Trim
22. Large LCD Panel

4. Rudder
2. Throttle . . . (MODE II) Elevator . . . (MODE I)
3. Elevator . . . (MODE II) Throttle . . . (MODE I)
1. Aileron
Neck Strap Hook
Soft Keys

Snap Roll Direction Switches (T9ZAP transmitter only)
Rubber grip (removed for stick tension adjustment)
RF Module
Data Transfer Trainer Cord DSC/Voltage measurement
Socket (with dust cap)
Battery cover
Battery Charge Jack (with dust cap)

*The instruction manual for the Futaba 9ZAP computerised helicopter system gives a fully annotated illustration of the transmitter functions – and for all programming sequences.*

stated otherwise, and the provision of a gyro is normal practice.

The typical airborne radio control system will comprise a receiver, battery and switch, aileron servo, elevator servo, throttle servo, pitch control servo, rudder servo (connected via the gyro), gyro, control amplifier and output trimmer. Where switchable variable-rate gyros are used, the receiver will need to have a minimum of six channel sockets.

Helicopter kits may specify as the radio control requirement four-channel and five-servo, but this is rather confusing as you will need more than the basic four-channel (function) outfit; it should be one that is specifically designated as a helicopter outfit. Obviously, the

higher-specification multi-purpose outfits, with facilities for fixed-wing powered models, gliders and helicopters, are suitable. Gyros may have their own independent battery supply, and in these cases they must also have a separate switch and charging socket.

*'Buddy box' training systems are most useful for helicopter training. If they have the facility to allow one control to be operated at a time by the student, this is a further advantage.*

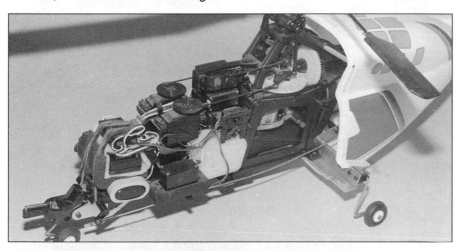

*In common with car construction kits, helicopter models also have body frames moulded, or machined, to accept the servos, gyros, receiver, battery, switch and, of course, the engine. All linkages are supplied; ball links are commonly used at the non-servo end and provide adjustment to the pushrod length.*

## Operation

Mode selection is probably more critical with helicopter flying than other forms of fixed-wing models. The Mode 1 and 2 arrangements are available as before, but Mode 3 is also used, by the present World Champion no less. Operating the 'cuddle box' with the three principal functions on one stick and the throttle control on the side of the transmitter case precludes the use of a transmitter tray, although a neck strap may be attached. Many helicopter flyers use a transmitter tray as they find being able to rest their wrists on the tray and holding the sticks between finger and thumb allows them greater accuracy of control. More than any other form of R/C flying, operating helicopters is a very personal thing and it is necessary to experiment to find the most suitable transmitter arrangements to suit individual styles.

Instructions in the owner's manual for programming all of the mixing, pitch and throttle curves, idle-up, throttle hold, gyro switching, autorotation settings, etc, on a computerised transmitter are complex. Indeed, they are impossible to understand until you comprehend the full functioning of the helicopter and how it operates. Before you can make sensible use of the facilities in a full-specification helicopter radio outfit you must either buy a book explaining the assembly, setting up and flying of helicopters, or seek the help and advice of an experienced helicopter pilot.

Having a 'buddy box' system where individual controls can be programmed to be operated by a pupil is of particular value to both teacher and learner. Being able to isolate the elevator, rudder and other controls allows the pupil to experience the cause and effect of

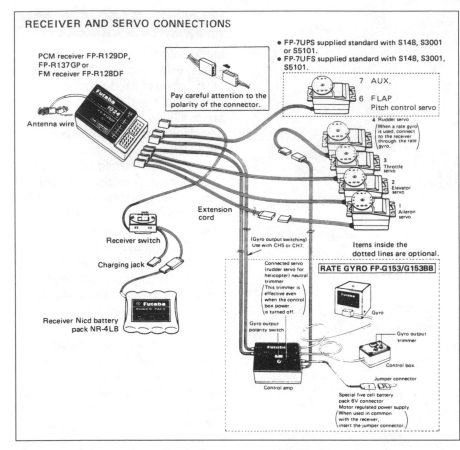

RECEIVER AND SERVO CONNECTIONS

*Radio outfit instructions (for helicopter types) will tell you how to incorporate a gyro stabiliser into the system. (Futaba Radio)*

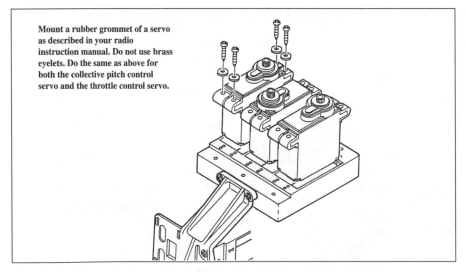

*Helicopter kits will illustrate the fitting of all the airborne radio components and the linkages to the controls.*

the different controls in turn, without having the complication of trying to operate all control functions and keep the model in the air.

## A special skill

Of all the modelling disciplines helicopter flying benefits most from the additional facilities and control options made available by computerised R/C equipment. For the serious helicopter enthusiast it really does make sense to purchase equipment with a good variety of programmable functions, even as the first outfit. For instance, the availability of alternative Mode 1 or 2 (or Mode 4 where the left and right-hand stick functions are transposed) and the aforementioned 'buddy box' system can prove to be important right from the beginning.

From this purchase it will be necessary to study the instruction books on the helicopter to be built and of the radio equipment until they are fully understood. This may well involve the additional purchase of technical books on the subject and instructional videos. Without a complete grasp of the subject the tyro helicopter flyer is unlikely to be successful in his attempts to become proficient in this branch of the hobby.

# Chapter 8

# The dream continues

Having seen so many developments in radio control modelling, having been involved in film and television work with R/C models, and having been fortunate enough to visit many parts of the world as a result of my hobby, it would be all too easy to become blasé about radio control. Far from it! When I'm out flying an R/C model I still occasionally look at it and think 'I'm controlling that' – it still gives me a sense of excitement and joy.

Improving standards of radio equipment has also led to a higher quality of model. When radio was less reliable than it is today there was a natural reluctance to spend many hours building and finishing a model which might be totally demolished in a few seconds as a result of a systems failure. Now, a modeller might spend over 2,000 hours producing an absolute masterpiece, then put it at the mercy of the elements, his skill and the reliability of the radio equipment. There is and always will be a slight risk that something may go wrong, either with the model or the radio, but it is that risk element that makes our hobby so exciting and demanding. If an engine never stopped or a servo never failed – or we never made a human mistake – it would be a lesser hobby.

## Choices

In the introduction I intimated that the cost of equipment and the amount of enjoyment obtained from its use were not related, and I am convinced that this is true. One of the hardest questions I am asked about radio control equipment are 'What make should I buy and what type – how many functions?', 'Computerised?', 'PCM or FM?', etc. There are no simple answers, as they depend so much on how much involvement modellers are likely to have in the hobby, whether they will be satisfied to stay with the relatively simple models or whether they will, quite quickly, want to progress to more advanced, competitive models. I say 'quite quickly' because radio equipment is improving constantly and there would be little point in buying a 'state-of-the-art' outfit now in the hope that you would still be getting the full benefit of it in four or five years' time – 'state of the art' will have moved on by then.

All that can be said to the beginner about purchasing an outfit is to go for one of the reputable manufacturers – their names will appear regularly in the model magazines – and check that there is a servicing agent in the country, preferably close at hand.

With regard to the number of functions, etc, required, aim for the middle of the road, five or six functions, possibly computerised, but no more advanced than that.

*Improved standards of radio equipment and engines have allowed the modeller to extend his horizons – but it is rare to become blasé about the 'magic' of remotely controlling a model.*

The possible exception is with helicopters, where the extra functions and facilities can be an advantage even at the beginning, providing that you take the trouble to read the instructions thoroughly, understand them, then get assistance in learning to fly.

As an aside, I would rate the helicopter as the most difficult of all R/C models to master, and it would be rash and foolish to spend many hundreds of pounds then attempt to fly the model on your own. There are good clubs around and there are also companies that offer individual training courses; they will save you money in the long run.

## Degrees of sophistication

### Simply does it – the 'Vimy' experience

Returning to the question of what degree of sophistication of radio control equipment is needed, a colleague and I were invited to participate in a prestigious competition in the United States of America for scale model aircraft. The model we made for this event was a scale replica of the 1919 Vickers 'Vimy', the first aircraft to fly the Atlantic non-stop, piloted by Alcock and Brown. It seemed an appropriate choice. Although I had plenty of radio equipment in the UK – too much in fact – it was not on a suitable frequency for operation in the USA, except for one outfit. This was an absolutely basic five-function outfit without any of the trimmings, not even rate switches or mixing controls. The only concession to the approach of the 21st century were the servo reversing switches.

Now, the 'Vimy' model was quite complex. It was a biplane, it had two engines, was reasonably large at 104 inches (2.6 metres) wing span, had a complement of

*'If you can't stand the heat, get out of the kitchen.' Yes, accidents do happen, aeroplanes fall out of the sky, cars crash into walls and even boats have been known to sink. It all helps to make it a more challenging and rewarding hobby.*

eight servos and used battery-backers. It was powered by two Laser 100 four-stroke engines. I opted to fit the basic five-function radio, although the plane had been test flown in the UK on a more 'glamorous' transmitter.

When we got to the American site of the scale contest I went to book in my transmitter and the model for the contest. The gentleman responsible for transmitter control was horrified.

'Are you going to fly that with this?' he asked, pointing to the aeroplane and transmitter.

'Certainly,' I replied, and left him standing open-mouthed.

The 'Vimy' was a delightful model to fly, but it was somewhat different from the average sports model. With such a nest of bracing wires, and thin wing sections that tended to warp – particularly in the Florida sunshine – the rigging was something of a put-it-together-and-

*The Vickers 'Vimy' was a complex model controlled by a simple radio control outfit – but with complex wiring systems and a battery backer!*

hope exercise. In fact, all the times I flew it I do not think that the trim was ever the same two flights in succession. Thus you flew it by the seat of your pants and the best programmable transmitter trim in the world would have been of no help in this respect.

On the test flight in the USA we had an engine go out because I had not tightened the glow plug (it is the silly things that usually get you), and with the downwind location of the model, with people and stands behind, there was just insufficient amount of elevator and rudder control to bring her round safely, as she was flying on the equivalent of full rates. Again, no amount of transmitter wizardry would have helped in that situation. Fortunately, we had a good bunch of modellers out there and they repaired it just in time for the contest.

The first flight was aborted because of suspected radio interference, but the second round flight went well. A fairly strong wind was blowing, which meant that I had to set the 'Vimy' slightly into the wind for a straight run, and that the downwind and upwind turns

were all different. Each manoeuvre required a different aileron and rudder input, to give a balanced and correct rate of turn, so a fixed-couple mix would have been no use in these instances. Full elevator control was needed at various points during the flight, so even if they had been available I would not have been able to use rate switches (not absolutely true – I might have switched to low-rate aileron on the fly-pasts).

No flaps were fitted, on the model or the full-size aircraft, and, of course, no retracts; indeed, no special functions whatsoever. It was our first international scale contest and we came about halfway up the leader board, so we were by no means disgraced – and all with a radio outfit, except for the extra servos and battery-backer, that could be purchased for around $150.

## Towards over-sophistication

It is also interesting to speculate how things will move in the other direction. A form of direction-finding employed by air forces

during the Second World War, and afterwards, consisted of a transmission of a narrow, powerful beam signal. When you knew you were somewhere near the beam, but still relatively uncertain of your position, you would switch on your receiver and listen on the earphones. Depending on which side of the beam you were positioned you would either get an 'A' signal (dot-dash) or an 'N' signal (dash-dot), and this gave you the information for which way to turn to bisect the beam. As you reached the opposite signal you would turn again and so keep making smaller and smaller corrections until you were accurately aligned with the beam and receiving a steady tone signal. Following the beam would direct you back to base, providing you were not flying a reciprocal course, and the beam would get narrower as you came towards the transmitter. There seems no reason why the model transmitter should not be programmed to transmit such a signal, and, with the assistance of an autopilot system, for the model to be capable of following the beam and homing into the signal. But perhaps we ought to consider the far-reaching consequences of such systems.

In Chapter 5 I stated that it would be wrong to consider programming out too many of our own control skills. Using eye/brain/hand co-ordination to instruct the radio control model to perform a series of manoeuvres is what our hobby is all about, not the entering of a series of instructions into a computer and watching the model perform – that is automation. How far we go along the path of programming the transmitter to perform certain functions will depend on the individual and what he or she wishes to achieve. I am sure that the manufacturers will be only too willing to provide the equipment to meet the demands of the operator – and they will often persuade the operator that he needs some device when he had never even thought of its use.

Competition is responsible for many of the advances in technology, but it is then up to the governing body of the competition sport to decide whether it is acceptable. For instance, in Formula 1 Grand Prix racing, traction control was introduced for the cars, then banned. In modelling we are seeing a similar problem. From the start an R/C car, given full power, will often slide sideways, but by fitting a gyro device the sideways movement can be eliminated, or at least restricted. Fair, or cheating? Aerobatic models can be programmed to carry out very consistent slow rolls, or enter a spin perfectly. Should such electronic aids be allowed in competition?

With the advent of return information, signalled from the model back to the operator, a whole new series of possibilities becomes available. Information on the speed of a model, battery state, height and climb or sink information for a contest glider, engine performance, precise location – all these could be available with existing technology, but do we want them – except for the one reason of winning competition?

Some might say that we already have all the radio control technology we need, but this will not stop the designers and manufacturers from developing new ideas and new 'selling gimmicks'. It would be nice to think that they will spend just as much time and effort on making the equipment ever more cost-effective.

There are, of course, commercial and military purposes for radio control, more likely referred to as remote control, although that covers a much wider scope, where special and automatic functions will be sought after, but this is not really the scope of this book. It is sad that model radio control equipment has already been put to unlawful and murderous use by terrorists, but it is difficult to prevent such uses.

## R/C on TV

On a more cheerful note, our systems are used extensively in the world of entertainment for stage and film work. Stage magicians such as Paul Daniels make good use of radio control in their acts, not to perpetrate deceit, but to create effects – including a pair of dancing ice skates!

*Filming with a model Boeing 767 for the television programme* Equinox, *appropriately on the subject of automated flying.*

*In the making of the TV series* Airline *a model 'Auster' was used to represent the full-size aircraft for snow scenes, where only a small area of the airfield was 'dressed' with artificial snow.*

For TV and film work it is often necessary to recreate the past, which would be impossible financially if done in the real, full-size world. Radio control models can be very useful in these circumstances. In *Airline*, a TV series in which I was involved, a number of DC3 'Dakota' aircraft were required. Part of the filming was carried out with the real aircraft – there are many DC3s still flying around the world, although they are over 50 years old – and part with models.

Radio control models are expendable and do not risk anyone's life, so can be used for the dangerous episodes – and other effects, too. So, when a DC3 had to be seen in a spin, or with its undercarriage collapsing on the ground, or, with an 'Auster' model, having to land on snow – in July – then models are called upon to recreate those episodes. The snow scene was particularly difficult as there was only a small area that was dressed with salt and foam to simulate the snow, and the landing direction, between quarter-scale fir trees, was crosswind. Such times can be exciting.

In another scene a DC3 had to crash into the roof of a farmhouse, in a very precise point on the roof. We used a model farmhouse with tiles stuck on the roof separately, together with the model 'Dak'. R/C flyers would like to think that they can fly a model accurately and position it exactly where a film director would require, but the size of the target area on this occasion was just a little too small. I am sure that we would have got the shot eventually, but only after crashing quite a few aeroplanes and demolishing a few farmhouses. In the end we compromised and 'flew' the DC3, suspended from a cable by clear nylon monofilament lines, into the precise position on the roof.

*Ten-foot wingspan model DC3 'Dakotas' were used in the filming . . .*

*. . . but full-size aeroplane parts were used for the farmhouse explosion scene.*

The next scene of the sequence showed the DC3 on top of the roof and on fire. Various old parts of aircraft were found, installed on the top of an old full-size farmhouse and set fire to, in a controlled way with pipes of various inflammable liquids and extinguishable at a command from the director. When the series was eventually shown on television a knowledgeable and experienced scale modeller watched this episode and commented, 'Of course, you could tell that the Dakota on the farmhouse was a model.' He assumed that they would not go to the trouble of putting a real aircraft on the roof of a real farmhouse, and therefore disbelieved what he saw on the screen. At such times you win!

## Robotics

Remote control, by the use of radio equipment, is not confined to boats, cars and aeroplanes. One area that may see much greater use of radio control systems in the future is in the development of robotics. Speaking of robots automatically conjures up a picture of an electro-mechanical form of a human being, but the term 'robotic' covers a vast field of industrial and recreational purposes. Industrialists may find applications in operating cranes, earth-movers, tractors – the possibilities are vast. Individuals could one day be mowing the lawn while sitting in a deck-chair, sipping a Martini and controlling the mower with his spare hand. Housewives – or husbands – could be helped in their household chores by a non-human, unpaid, prepared-to-work-24-hours-a-day, non-answering-back, radio-controlled domestic help; although there might still be the argument of whose turn it was to charge the batteries.

Military applications, using ever more sophisticated forms of control, will have the benefit of removing the risk of human involvement in certain applications. They may also assist in helping to pinpoint targets and allowing weapons to be accurately positioned – hopefully on military installations. That the use of radio control targets saves the military services a vast amount of money is already a fact. Using purpose-designed R/C aircraft for target practice and surveillance work has reduced the costs of utilising full-size machines for these purposes. With the advent of miniature model gas turbine engines, the military application in target drones becomes more acceptable as this makes them suitable for testing heat-seeking missiles. There is no reason why more R/C-operated surface vehicle targets, on land and sea, should not be employed. Using static targets for simulations of 'moving' battle conditions cannot be very instructive.

## Indoors and out

However, our main concern here is with the recreational aspects of radio control applications, and here, too, there are many openings. Already we have seen 'fire-breathing' model dragons, robots and remote-controlled animals. Model railway enthusiasts have not been slow to see the potential of using R/C for the operation of their locomotives, track points and signalling. Used on the larger gauges of model railways (O gauge and above) radio control will probably be introduced in the smaller scales as miniaturisation becomes widely available. Some of the more experienced model railway enthusiasts obviously find it difficult to accept fully the 'remote'

advantages of radio operation, and continue to accompany their locomotives as they move around the track.

True miniaturisation, when the receiver, servos and battery have a total weight of only a few grams, will open up the possibilities of indoor modelling tremendously. Indoor R/C flying in village-hall-sized rooms will be possible, table-top cars and race tracks will be, literally, in-house – the potential for miniature scale models is almost limitless.

Heavier-than-air models have been operated outdoors and indoors for many years. The spectacle of indoor pylon racing of model aeroplanes with miniature 0.3 cc IC engines is something that was only a dream a few years back. Now, at the Grand Hall, Olympia, during the Model Engineer Exhibition, you can witness three or four R/C models racing around a two pylon course at speeds of up to 60 mph (94 kph). At the same exhibition you could witness the slowest of all R/C model aircraft, a gas-filled model 'Blimp' airship, powered by small electric-motor-driven propellers. At such exhibitions you have a chance to see most of the aspects of radio control models, as there are also displays of boats and car racing.

## Future developments

I have already mentioned the need for a dual frequency radio system where the standby frequency would automatically cut in if there was interference on the primary frequency. Also mentioned was the introduction of synthesised frequencies and the discontinuation of single frequency crystals. If a transmitter could be programmed, when switched on, to first scan the frequency band and ascertain whether there are

*There are still plenty of challenges left for radio control enthusiasts. Gas turbine engines now make possible true jet models – for boats and cars, too!*

any other transmissions on the initially selected frequency, all before any RF transmission occurs, this would be a great safety device. It would, in effect, be an in-built frequency monitor. If the transmitter then automatically moved on to the next available free frequency and indicated that it was safe to transmit, it would provide a secure system of operation.

Extending the system to carry out a similar procedure during operation, for example if someone accidentally switched a 'standard' transmitter to that frequency, it would again move on to the next clear frequency. If all operators were to use such a system there would be no need to indicate, by pennants and pegs, the frequency being used, as it would,

*Experimental aircraft, such as this Boeing tilt rotor, will require all the help possible from modern radio equipment and the skills of the operator.*

*Re-creation of world events, records, contests and wartime exploits is possible with the help of radio control.*

theoretically at least, be impossible for two transmitters and receivers to stay on the same frequency. For model meetings involving multi-disciplines it would be necessary to group the transmitter frequencies within sub-divided frequency bands to ensure a fair split of available frequencies.

Whatever systems are devised for frequency transmission in the future, anything that obviates the risk of two transmitters operating on a common frequency, or allows automatic switching to a secondary frequency in the event of interference, will represent a great step forward in safety.

Fibre optics is another area where there is room for development for transmitting the signals within the model. Wire

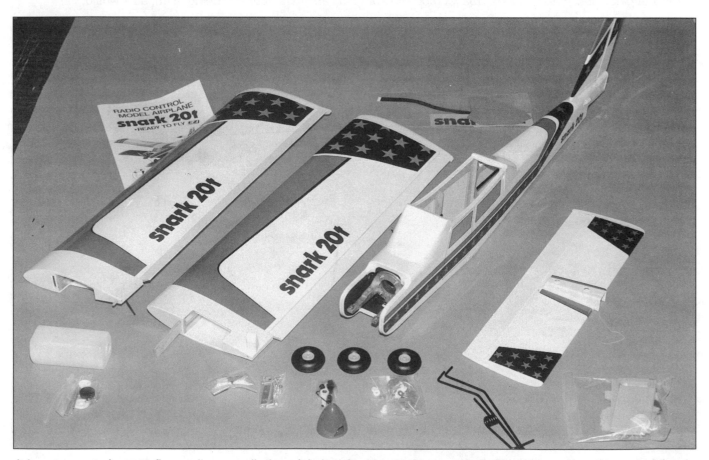

*It is not easy to learn to fly a radio-controlled model aircraft without tuition, so if you have to go along this route it is probably better to purchase an 'ARTF' (Almost Ready to Fly) model of suitable trainer design – no 'Spitfires' please! …*

leads, our normal way of transferring the signals from the receiver to the servos, are not ideal over long distances. They can suffer from feedback and require chokes to prevent this; there is a diminution of signal strength if the wires are too thin; and the wires can act as the aerial in certain circumstances, robbing the receiver of the transmitter signal. Fibre optics may become commercially available in the future – they have already been used for film models.

Crystal ball gazing about the radio control developments to come is fun, and it seems difficult to imagine the many radical breakthroughs yet to be made, but no doubt the designers and manufacturers have other ideas. I would simply make one plea – for every hour spent on designing new 'bells, whistles and knobs', I would hope that they will spend at least

*… Boats and cars offer a much higher chance of success for the lone hand.*

as long working on improvements in equipment reliability. It is already very reliable, but needs to become ultra-reliable. When the manufacturers have played their part, we must also make the effort to make the models safe and more reliable, for not all of the general public are as enamoured with the hobby as we may be, and would gladly find a reason for having it banned. We must do everything in our power to avoid them having this excuse.

I am reminded of Nevil Shute's comment in his autobiography: 'Aircraft do not crash of themselves. They come to grief because men are foolish, or vain, or lazy, or irresolute, or reckless.' This applies equally to model aircraft.

To return to the more mundane, I once wrote in a magazine that building models was challenging and rewarding and that radio control was simply the means of controlling them. There was no point in building the radio equipment yourself because (at the time, for tax reasons) there were no savings and, anyway, it gave no enjoyment. The letters that followed corrected my views in no uncertain way. Of course there was satisfaction and pleasure in building the radio control equipment, for some modellers just as much, if not more, than building the model. In truth, it would be very difficult and time-consuming to build a full radio control system 'from scratch'. To build the servo mechanics would certainly represent a labour of love. There are still assembly kits on the market for transmitters, receivers, speed controllers and electronic switches; these are competitive in price and work well.

We use re-chargeable nicad batteries, and now the nickel metal hydride cells to a great extent in our equipment. The new 'green'

*Living the dream. There is no shortage of aircraft types to model. The simplified 'Hyperfly' helicopter (it doesn't have a working tail rotor) is within the flying capabilities and price range of most modellers. Or you can fly off water or snow with simple sports models or detailed scale replicas (below and opposite).*

cells are said to offer further advantages over the standard nicads, being free of any toxic elements, having a better capacity performance and protection against polarity reversal. All good news and a further step in the right direction.

If there was to be a major development in re-chargeable batteries, and by that I mean an increase of efficiency (power-to-weight ratio) in the order of 200 to 300 per cent, R/C modelling would

be revolutionised – and many other aspects of life as well. We already have electric-powered fixed-wing and rotary-wing aircraft, boats and cars, but seriously improved battery power would nearly eliminate the IC engine from many classes of these models. The radio control equipment itself would not be unduly affected, although it would reduce the battery complement weight for both the transmitter and the receiver/servos.

## Brand loyalty

As a magazine editor and author on radio control subjects I have to keep abreast of developments, and as a result buy, and in some cases have to test, all types and makes of equipment. This is not something that I would recommend to R/C modellers. Temptation to buy the latest equipment will be there, whether we need it or not, and it is the manufacturer's job to advertise their products as the best and most indispensable that there is on the market. It may well be true. One manufacturer may get a technical edge on another for a short time, but it is unlikely, if the new product or design represents an important development, that one manufacturer will have that technical lead for long; others will come along with their version.

Reputable R/C equipment manufacturers are here to stay and will give you good product items and servicing arrangements. Their own products are compatible with one another, as far as is possible; in other words a PCM transmitter will also have PPM transmission so that it can be used with PPM (FM) receivers. However, manufacturers normally use different plugs, sockets and wiring systems to each other, and the equipment is not compatible between makes – or rarely so. Once you have started to use a particular make of equipment and are satisfied with the performance, keep with that manufacturer. There are few things more frustrating than wanting to instal some item of radio equipment in a model, usually in a hurry, and finding that you have the receiver from one make, servos from another, switch harness from a third and possibly a battery pack with a totally unrecognisable socket. Brand loyalty makes good economic sense with radio control.

## Living the dream

Perhaps reading this book, assuming you have reached this far, has given you some enthusiasm to get started in radio control modelling. If it has, I would like to make some suggestions of how you can go about taking those first steps – and avoiding a few mistakes and costly errors.

It is possible to learn to operate any of the radio control models mentioned in this book without any more tuition than you can gain from the reading of books on the subject, then going out to practise. For boats this is not at all difficult as the speeds are generally slow and will give you ample time to make steering correction. For cars, too, you can start with the less expensive two-function off-road vehicles, learn the basics of steering the cars and servicing them before, if you so wish, going on to the more advanced racing cars.

When considering fixed-wing aeroplanes and helicopters, however, the problems in learning to fly entirely on your own, or with the help of an inexperienced assistant, are very considerable. Put simply, the first time you take-off you have to learn to fly the model – and to land it – in a matter of minutes. I can think of no equivalent hobby or sport where you are thrown into the 'deep end' with so much at stake. It is not an impossible task – the pioneers of R/C flying had to do it that way – but you will only succeed if you have a very strong will and are prepared to break and have to repair many models.

*Prefer wind power? Slope soarers are great fun in the summer months – the B-52 'Big Buff' looks impressive.*

To avoid such disappointments there are two alternatives: you can get private tuition, from a number of companies specialising in this, or you can join a club or group and be helped by more experienced modellers. Most will opt for the latter, as it is certainly less expensive and may well be more convenient; the private tuition may involve travelling long distances to the training venue. The disadvantages of a club training system is that there may in fact be no system and the tuition periods may be infrequent and with different instructors on each occasion.

In a well-regulated world every club would have a properly organised training scheme available for beginners and learners, with their own dual control training models for the use of club members. However, it is not a perfect world, we are all amateurs trying to enjoy our hobby, and may not be the best of organisers and arrangers. As a result the standards of clubs, with regard to flying sites, facilities, number of members, etc, will vary enormously. Pay them a visit and see what the club or group is like and how it will suit you – and how you will fit in with the other members.

It is not for the training facilities alone, however, that one should consider becoming a member of a group sharing a common activity. It is the comradeship, pleasure in taking part in discussion about the hobby, seeing what your fellow modellers are doing and learning from it and, in general, sharing your activities. There are other positive advantages in being a member of a group: you will have the use of the modelling sites available and almost certainly have insurance cover as part of the subscription fee.

*Finally, the futuristic-looking 'Starship' gave the designer of the prototype a few problems – and the model designer too!*

Whether you belong to a club or not it is absolutely essential that you have good insurance cover, ie Third Party accident insurance. It is unlikely that you will be able to obtain insurance for damage to the model or radio equipment, the risk being too high, but to cover yourself against damage to persons or property is a must. Without it you are liable for any costs awarded to the injured person or damaged property to the extent that legally all your valuables and your house could be taken in payment. It is not worth the risk.

There are several companies specialising in model insurance. One is MAP Insurance, details of which are available from Nexus, Boundary Way, Hemel Hempstead, Herts HP2 7ST (01442 66551); this company also operates the Model Pilots Association, an organisation aimed at helping individual modellers with meetings, training schemes and other activities.

So have much pleasure from your hobby, and please remember that it is a hobby. It is about enjoyment and not to be taken too seriously – except where safety is concerned.

# Postscript

Over ten years ago, when editing the *Radio Control Models & Electronics* magazine, I included a joke article to coincide with the April issue. The idea was to present an idea in serious form although it was an 'impossible' concept. The suggestion was that a method had been found of transmitting brainwaves direct to a radio control-style model and, by so doing, eliminating the need for a conventional radio transmitter.

Illustrations to the article included the author's son wearing a suitably futuristic-looking headband, complete with aerial, and a few boffin-like characters standing around and looking impressed. Obviously, it was all intended as a bit of fun and we didn't really expect to fool any of the modellers into believing that this equipment had actually been produced, or was feasible.

Indeed, the modellers were not fooled, but it was with some surprise that we found out that the military authorities were more than a little interested in our supposed activities. Where had we obtained our information? Did we have any contacts with military establishments? How far had our experiments progressed? In their eyes we were obviously working along parallel lines to some of their own research, and we were being viewed with deep suspicion.

How much further any military authorities have gone towards developing a practical 'thought transference guidance system' I do not know; it may be that one is already operating. But whether such a system will ever be practical on a commercial modelling basis is anybody's guess; the mind literally boggles at the thought of the potential problems to be solved.

Until there is a major breakthrough in the means of transmitting information from our brain to the models we will have to be satisfied with the existing methods and systems. Perhaps we will have a different physical means of operating the controls whereby, if we are driving a racing car, we sit in a cockpit more resembling a full-size machine. The same could apply to an aeroplane where you might sit in a 'fly-seat' with a joy-stick, rudder pedals and a throttle positioned at your side.

'Virtual reality', ie sophisticated simulation, may be thought to be capable of taking over the role of radio control models. After all, you can sit in the comfort of your home, 'drive', 'fly' or 'sail' your machine and have the reality of controlling it from the correct position, not from a remote location. You can programme the simulator for pretty well any condition you will find in the real car, plane or boat, but – and it is a very big but – you do not have the hands-on experience of preparing the models, testing them, operating them and, of course, the friendship and communication with fellow modellers. Simulators can be very useful in the areas of basic training and for fine-tuning of control techniques at a later stage, but they are not an end in themselves.

Radio control models, in their present forms, are here for a long time yet. If you have not experienced the enjoyment and satisfaction to be derived from the hobby, you should start right now.

# Appendix 1

# Glossary of terms & abbreviations

Abbreviations are used to a high degree in equipment instruction books and manuals, also in magazine articles and books. To the novice this can be incomprehensible gibberish, until the meanings of the abbreviations are understood. Although there is no standardisation of these 'shorthand' terms, the following list includes generally accepted meanings.

## General

| | |
|---|---|
| F/S | Fail-Safe |
| R/C | Radio Control |
| Rx | Receiver |
| SMT | Surface Mounting Technology |
| Tx | Transmitter |

## Frequencies

| | |
|---|---|
| MHz | Megahertz, as for transmission frequency, eg 35.020MHz |
| AM | Amplitude Modulation |
| FM | Frequency Modulation |
| IF | Intermediate Frequency |
| PPM | Pulse Position Modulation (same as FM) |
| PCM | Pulse Code Modulation |
| RF | Radiated Frequency |
| Syn | Synthesised frequency system |
| Xtal | Crystal (for frequency control) |

## Modes

| | |
|---|---|
| A or AIR | An R/C outfit suitable for aeroplane (power or glider) use |
| H or HE | For helicopter use |

## Channels/functions

| | |
|---|---|
| 4, 5, 6, etc. | Normally the number of channels or functions available |
| A, AIL or AILE | Aileron channel |
| AUX | Auxiliary channels |
| E, ELE or ELEV | Elevator channel |
| F or FLP | Flap channel |
| G, GER or GEAR | Undercarriage retract channel |
| R, RUD or RUDD | Rudder channel |
| T, THR or THRO | Throttle channel |

## Servo control setting

| | |
|---|---|
| AST | Adjustable Servo Throw |
| ATV | Adjustable Travel Volume |
| D/R | Dual Rate |
| DSC | Direct Servo Control |
| EPA | End Point Adjustment |
| EXP | Exponential |

## Servos

| | |
|---|---|
| kg/cm | Output torque of servo |
| LIN | Linear |
| NORM/REV | Normal or Reverse rotation of servo |
| sec/60 degrees | Operating speed of servo |
| VTR | Variable Trace Ratio (soft centre) |

## Receiver

| | |
|---|---|
| DC | Dual Conversion |
| ABC | Anti-Blocking and Cross modulation |
| ABC&W | Anti-Blocking and Cross modulation and windows |

## Electrical

| | |
|---|---|
| BATT | Battery |
| LED | Light Emitting Diode |
| LCD | Liquid Crystal Display |
| mAh | Milli-Amp-Hour |
| V | Volts |
| MA | Milli-Amps current drain |

# Appendix 2
# Computer technology terms and programming

With the introduction of more computerised radio outfits, the use of abbreviations and programming terms becomes less and less standardised. Each manufacturer will have their own symbols to use with the programming models, and these have to be learned from the operator's manual. The method of entering the System Menu Contents will also vary, although, for computer-literate modellers, the process will be fairly obvious.

How much information is displayed on the transmitter and the degree to which abbreviations are used, will depend on the size of the incorporated LCD screen. In general terms, the more functions and facilities incorporated in the system, the larger the LCD, allowing more information to be displayed at any given setting. For example, the Futaba 1024Z system is at the top of the range, is suitable for all types of aircraft (and surface vehicles), has multi-mixings potential and trim and mix facilities that are switchable during operation of the model. In other words, it is a high-tech, state-of-the-art outfit with all the functions one would expect from an advanced system for advanced models and modellers.

To accommodate this power, the PCM 1024Z system has four levels of operation: the Home Menu, the System Menu, the Model Menu and the Condition Menus.

The Home Menu appears when the system is first turned on, and displays such items as battery

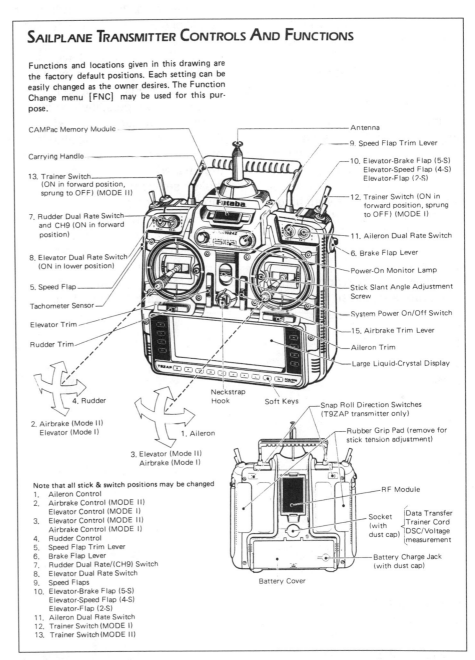

**SAILPLANE TRANSMITTER CONTROLS AND FUNCTIONS**

Functions and locations given in this drawing are the factory default positions. Each setting can be easily changed as the owner desires. The Function Change menu [FNC] may be used for this purpose.

CAMPac Memory Module

Carrying Handle

13. Trainer Switch (ON in forward position, sprung to OFF) (MODE II)

7. Rudder Dual Rate Switch and CH9 (ON in forward position)

8. Elevator Dual Rate Switch (ON in lower position)

5. Speed Flap

Tachometer Sensor

Elevator Trim

Rudder Trim

4. Rudder

2. Airbrake (Mode II) Elevator (Mode I)

3. Elevator (Mode II) Airbrake (Mode I)

1. Aileron

Antenna
9. Speed Flap Trim Lever
10. Elevator-Brake Flap (5-S) Elevator-Speed Flap (4-S) Elevator-Flap (2-S)
12. Trainer Switch (ON in forward position, sprung to OFF) (MODE I)
11. Aileron Dual Rate Switch
6. Brake Flap Lever
Power-On Monitor Lamp
Stick Slant Angle Adjustment Screw
System Power On/Off Switch
15. Airbrake Trim Lever
Aileron Trim
Large Liquid-Crystal Display

Neckstrap Hook    Soft Keys
Snap Roll Direction Switches (T9ZAP transmitter only)
Rubber Grip Pad (remove for stick tension adjustment)
RF Module
Socket (with dust cap) — Data Transfer / Trainer Cord / DSC/Voltage measurement
Battery Charge Jack (with dust cap)
Battery Cover

Note that all stick & switch positions may be changed
1. Aileron Control
2. Airbrake Control (MODE II) Elevator Control (MODE I)
3. Elevator Control (MODE II) Airbrake Control (MODE I)
4. Rudder Control
5. Speed Flap Trim Lever
6. Brake Flap Lever
7. Rudder Dual Rate/(CH9) Switch
8. Elevator Dual Rate Switch
9. Speed Flaps
10. Elevator-Brake Flap (5-S) Elevator-Speed Flap (4-S) Elevator-Flap (2-S)
11. Aileron Dual Rate Switch
12. Trainer Switch (MODE I)
13. Trainer Switch (MODE II)

*The Futaba transmitter in its T9ZAP form for sailplane operation – see also the chapter on Helicopters for the similar transmitter arranged for helicopter operation.*

voltage, trim positions, one or more timers and other functions. The top level display is what is normally displayed during operation.

The System Menu is the next level down, and is used to choose and call up the items that apply to all model set-ups stored within the PCM 1024Z transmitter. This menu includes such items as Model Select (which chooses which model set-up to use), Copy Model and Copy Condition, User Name inputting, Switch Setting and other items.

The Model Menu is next, containing unique information about each model stored within the PCM 1024Z's memory. Within this menu are settings that pertain to a particular model, which of course, can vary for each different model. For example, the Model Menu contains the Servo Reversing function, which may be different for each model stored.

Finally, the Condition Menus, which are customised to the different types of models that the PCM 1024Z system will accommodate: Airplane, Helicopter and Sailplane (the three Sailplane menus are further broken into the categories of five wing servos, four wing servos and two wing servos). In the Condition Menus, you may set up throws, mixing functions and other items that vary with flight conditions but are associated with one model set-up.

The PCM 1024ZA allows you to proceed directly to the menu that you need, bypassing those that do not need any inputs, instead of forcing the owner to proceed through a single, complicated loop, one menu at a time, on the way to the desired setting. This system makes setting up models both rapid and simple.

Familiarity with the transmitter and operating manual will improve the ability of the owner to program precisely the requirements of the model for varying conditions. However, it must be emphasised that to make full use of such technically advanced equipment, two other ingredients are needed. The radio installation, servos, linkages and hinging must be to a high standard, otherwise the precise control offered by the equipment will be lost.

It is also essential to be able to fly (drive or sail) the model accurately so that repeatability of manoeuvres will allow you to program the trims, mixes and special features sensibly. In other words, the equipment will not act as a substitute for poor operating skills, but it will allow you to make better use of high skill standards. To program the trims and other facilities accurately will require a lot of patience, practise and perseverance; it also makes the assumption that the life of the model will be long enough to be able to carry out this degree of 'fine-tuning'.

# Appendix 3

# Starting on the computer trail

There is no doubt that, for the generations not schooled in the use and understanding of computer technology, the introduction of computerisation into radio control equipment came as something of a shock. For the younger modeller the computerised outfit holds no surprises or fears, but it has to be remembered that the average age of modellers is much nearer to 60 years than 20. Manufacturers have already found that the programming systems originally introduced on video recorders were incomprehensible to many users, and as a result the more abstruse functions were never operated.

As a result of previous experience, and of ignorance, many modellers have resisted the purchase of computer R/C outfits because of the fear that they will not be able to understand them – and of making a fool of themselves. This is a pity, as modern equipment and the enlightened attitude of most of the program writers brings the present-day outfits within the understanding of mere mortals. Certainly there are still problems in describing the precise purpose of the many and varied functions, but this is a limitation of our written language and should not be confused with the ability to program the functions. I often wonder how the Japanese manage to define the systems, functions and programming when using the Japanese alphabet – perhaps it is a superior method to the use of the Western alphabet!

Until recently, computerised radio outfits have been synonymous with complex systems, often with six or more channels and high costs. Now we have the introduction of lower-cost, entry-level outfits providing more modest facilities but including computerisation and programming. One such system is the Hitec Flash 5 outfit, which has five channels, computer controlling and simplified programming. To this extent it is a useful example for explaining the basic programming system of a computerised outfit and, hopefully, by describing the methods used, will help to de-mystify the operation of this form of radio control. It will become commonplace in the future.

The system has FM (PPM) transmission and not PCM as is more usually associated with the computerised outfits. The other features are as follows:

### Transmitter

Four/five-channel microprocessor design
Two-model memory capability
In-flight timer and alarm
Changeable from MODE II to MODE I stick configuration
Low battery warning signal for transmitter
'End point' adjustment for channels 1 to 4
Dual rate switches for aileron and elevator

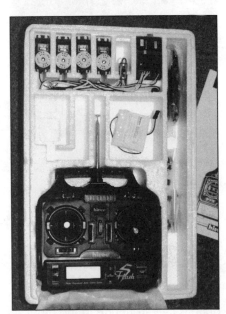

*The Hitec Flash 5 is supplied with an FM dual conversion receiver, four servos and accessories, nicad batteries, switch and charger (not shown).*

*A view of the transmitter you won't normally see – unless you are changing the stick mode arrangement.*

Exponential rates for channels 1 to 4
Trim memory for channels 1 to 4
Trim reset function (to factory defaults)
Three preset mixing functions (AIL/RUD, ELEVON, V-TAIL)
Master data reset function (to factory defaults)
Channel 5 retract landing gear switch
Trainer jack and switch
Power supply: 9.6 volt AA nicad pack, internal
Power consumption: 200MA

Standard Hitec single or dual conversion FM receivers can be used with the transmitter and it may be possible to operate it with other receivers, but this would have to be checked out and tested. A variety of Hitec servos and battery packs are available for use with the Flash 5, the standard outfit is supplied fully nicaded (rechargeable batteries) and with four servos and a charger. Frequencies in the 35, 36, 40, 41, 60 and 72MHz bands are available. Plug-in crystals are available for use within each frequency band.

*The Flash 5 transmitter has rate switches, channel 5 and trainer switch on the top panels, and three programming keys, the on/off switch, frequency crystal socket and LCD on the lower panel. There are electronic trims for the four principal functions. The rear of the transmitter has the socket for the 'buddy box' lead, the battery cover and housing for spare frequency crystals. The servos are standard HS-422 double-oilite-bearing types.*

Channel assignments are conventional with channel 1 Aileron, 2 Elevator, 3 Throttle, 4 Rudder and 5 for retracts. Although the transmitter can be supplied in Mode 1 or Mode 2 configuration, it can be changed quite easily from one to the other; the manual details these procedures.

### Digital trims

The Flash radio system features electronic, digitally controlled trim switches as opposed to conventional mechanically operated trim levers. This digital trim feature allows for very precise trim movements that are just not possible with the mechanical arrangement.

Setting the trims is quite similar to conventional radios with the exception that you will hear a short beep for each input, either plus or minus, to let you know that a change has been made. After the initial trimming-out flight, all you have to do is land the plane and save the trim settings in the memory.

## System overview

In order to take full advantage of the Flash radio system programming, it is necessary to become familiar with the input keys that make this all possible. The input operation requires the use of the following keys and switches on the transmitter:

The LCD display
The three main input keys (UP, DN/TIMER, CUT/SAVE)
The Rudder (channel 4) trim switch
The Aileron (channel 1) trim switch
The main power switch

The Flash has two main menu programs to select from when setting up your model(s), with each menu having separate methods of access to a particular menu. This prevents the accidental editing of programs in the incorrect 'mode'.

The first menu that needs to be accessed is called the 'INITIAL MODE' menu, and is comprised of the following sub-routines:

Mode configuration (Mode I or Mode II)
Flight timer settings
Aileron/Rudder mixing activation (on) or de-activation (off)
Elevon mixing activation (on) or de-activation (off)
V-Tail mixing activation (on) or de-activation (off)
Data memory save
Data memory reset (to factory defaults)

It is through this menu that the process of customising the radio to suit the needs of a particular aircraft begins.

Once the input for the initial mode program is completed and everything has been saved in the memory, it is time to access the 'MAIN EDIT MODE' menu, in which are made the basic servo adjustments required to make your model fly correctly. Use the same transmitter keys and switches that were used in the INITIAL MODE menu.

Within the MAIN EDIT MODE program it will be possible to access the following sub-routines:

'End point' adjustment (EPA)
Exponential rate adjustment
Dual rate adjustment (Flash 5 only)
Servo reversing
Trim memory
Trim memory reset
Aileron/Rudder mixing
Data save to memory

Note: The Aileron/Rudder mixing sub-routine will only appear on the screen if you have selected that mixing function in the INITIAL MODE program. Otherwise the menu goes directly to the 'Data save' sub-routine after trim memory reset.

## Additional features

When the transmitter is first switched on the voltage reading appears on the LCD screen; if it reads below 9.4 volts the batteries should be re-charged. Voltage is monitored constantly and when it drops to 9.2 volts an audible alarm will sound; it is then time to land before the voltage drops below a safe level.

An 'engine cut' feature allows the engine to be positively cut (from the operation of the CUT/SAVE input button) at times

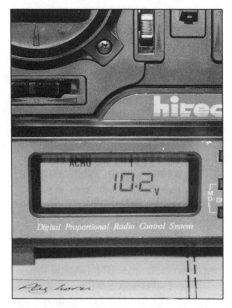

*When first switched on the transmitter LCD will probably indicate 11 volts or over; this is normal and will drop to 10 volts plus after being used for 10 minutes or so.*

of emergency; the normal idle setting is not affected.

Available as an optional extra is the trainer system cord, which can be plugged into the transmitter at the 'Master' end and into the 'Student' socket on a similar transmitter. A switch on the 'Master' transmitter is held over when control is passed to the 'Student' transmitter; it is impossible for this transmitter to be accidentally switched on and used for transmitting when the cord is in place.

## Programming the Flash computer system

The following instructions are taken from the Operation Manual to give an idea of how the selection and programming is achieved. These are not the full complement of instructions, but should illustrate the general methods and show that it is within the capabilities of the 'ordinary' modeller to operate and understand the process.

## Model selection

The Hitec Flash offers the modeller the ability to store information for two separate models in a non-volatile memory. As a safety feature, the Flash has a separate access procedure to recall the model you wish to either begin flying or to bring up for programming purposes. To make the model selection, simply depress both the DN/TIMER key and the CUT/SAVE key simultaneously. While holding both down, slide the power switch to the ON position (up). An 'SL', with either a small '1' or '2' (for model selection) above it, should now be displayed on the LCD screen.

To make your model selection, if necessary press the CUT/SAVE key once to change the model number. Pressing the CUT/SAVE key again will return you to the previous model number. After you

have made your model selection, simply turn off the transmitter and this model number will be stored in the default memory until you repeat this process and change it. Remember that all programming changes from this point on affect only the model you currently have selected; the other model memory will not be affected.

LCD display:
a. While pressing both DN/TIMER and CUT/SAVE keys down, turn main power ON.
b. Press CUT/SAVE key to select the model desired.
c. Turn the main power switch OFF and ON again to activate the model selected.

## Initial mode programming

As the title indicates, the INITIAL MODE menu is used to define how you wish the transmitter to operate and to designate which mixing operations you wish to employ.

This needs to be defined prior to accessing the MAIN EDIT menu since selections made in this programming mode affect the programming decisions in the MAIN EDIT menu.

To access the INITIAL MODE menu it will be necessary to have the transmitter turned off; verify that the power switch is in the down position. Next, while depressing both the UP key and the DN/TIMER key simultaneously, slide the power switch to the ON position (up). The LCD should now display the message ACRO plus a small number to verify which model you have selected to work on. If this message does not appear on your screen, turn the power off and repeat the process, making sure that both the UP key and the DN/TIMER key are being pressed at the same time. We are now ready to begin the programming process.

The manual then continues with a description of the stick mode change and on to:

*When switched on with the DN TIMER and CUT keys depressed, an 'SL' should be seen on the screen and '1' (for model selection); activate the selection.*

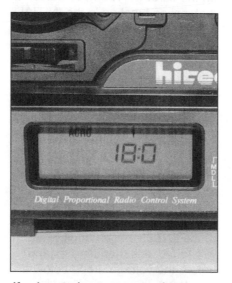

*If, when trying to access the INITIAL MODE, you don't press both keys simultaneously you will start the timer (set, in this instance, at 18 minutes) – try again.*

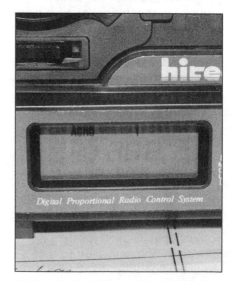

*This is the display when both keys are correctly depressed and the power switched ON.*

## Countdown timer feature

Your Flash radio is equipped with a built-in timer to alert you to any number of situations such as low fuel, low receiver battery or even task completion. To set the timer, press the UP key until the time indicator starts flashing. The factory default for the timer is set at 10 minutes, but you may change this to as much as 30 minutes or to as low as 1 minute.

To change the timer, locate the Rudder (channel 4) trim switch. To increase the amount of time on the timer, press the right side of the trim switch; to decrease the amount of time, press the left side of the trim switch. In either case, you will hear a beep for each minute of time added or subtracted from the timer.

Once again you need to save this setting. Press the UP key or the DN/TIMER key until the SA (save) message is seen on the display, then press the CUT/SAVE key and your timer information is now in memory.

LCD display:
a. While pressing both UP and DN/TIMER keys down, turn main power switch ON.
b. Press either UP or DN/TIMER key until the display shows the timer setting menu.
c. Use CH 4 trim to input time value.
d. Go to the INITIAL MODE SAVE menu by using either UP or DN/TIMER key and press CUT/SAVE key to save the input data.

## Mixing functions

The Flash radio systems offer you a choice of three separate mixing functions: Aileron/Rudder, Elevon or V-Tail. While still in the INITIAL MODE menu, press the UP key until you come to the first of the three mixing options; this will be the AIL-RUD option. Just above this will be a flashing ON or OFF message. If you wish to engage this mixing option and the OFF message is flashing, press the CUT/SAVE key once and the message will then read ON. Scroll with the UP key until you see the SA (save) message and press the CUT/SAVE key. The transmitter is now set up for Aileron/Rudder mixing.

The other two mixing options, Elevon and V-Tail, are activated in the same manner as the AIL/RUD mix. After selecting one or other of the mixes, remember to save them in the memory. Please note that you may select only one mixing option per model. That means that if you designate a model as having one mixing, the other two mixing options are automatically turned off.

*Select the Aileron/Rudder mix by pressing the UP key, and it will signify the mix as being OFF. Press the CUT/SAVE key and it will change to ON. Save this if you want the mix retained.*

## LCD display

a. While pressing both UP and DN/TIMER keys down, turn main power switch ON.

b. Press either UP or DN/TIMER key until the display shows the mixing menu.

c. Select mixing ON/OFF by CUT/SAVE key.

d. Go to the INITIAL MODE SAVE menu by using either UP or DN/TIMER key and press CUT/SAVE key to save the input data.

Instructions are then given on re-setting to the original factory default settings and how to carry out visual checks of the transmitter and servo for the correct programming.

## Main Edit Mode programming

In this mode the modeller can perform all the necessary servo adjustments required prior to taking the aeroplane out on its initial flight. This includes setting the 'end points', exponential rates, servo reversing, etc. The Flash radio system allows these adjustments to be performed quickly and easily in any model. Both the novice and the expert pilot will easily grasp the fundamentals of customising the programs to suit their flying needs. Take a moment to review the MAIN EDIT MODE flow chart and you will see how the menu selection process works.

Because you will be able to see the servos respond as soon as you input the data, it is suggested that you install the radio gear into the model you wish to set up at this time. If this is not feasible, continue with the receiver and servos set out in front of you and watch the results of the data input.

To access the MAIN EDIT MODE menu, you will need to exit the INITIAL MODE menu. To do this, simply turn off the radio, let the LCD screen go blank, then turn the radio back on. The screen should now prominently display the transmitter voltage once again.

Next, with the transmitter still ON, press both the UP key and the DN/TIMER key simultaneously. You should now be in the MAIN EDIT MODE menu with the EPA routine now showing on the screen. You should turn on the receiver at this point to see the full effect of your programming.

## End Point Adjustment (EPA)

The End Point Adjustment function allows you to determine the amount of travel a servo will have to each side of the centre position. This will ensure that you do not over-rotate the servo, risking damage to the control linkage or to the servo itself. It also allows you to set up control surfaces that are 'mild' (decreased servo travel) for the novice pilot or to set up extremely sensitive control surfaces for the expert pilot by

*Enter the MAIN EDIT MODE by depressing, simultaneously, the UP and DN/TIMER keys, then select the channel required, in this case 1; the EPA travel shows the factory default of 100%.*

*Move the Aileron (channel 1) stick to the right, then, using the Aileron trim switch, increase or decrease the amount of servo movement (shown here increased by 14%). Have the airborne system switched on to verify the movement*

*Then do the same for the left-hand Aileron movement, and save the setting.*

extending the servo travel range. Adjustment of any one channel can be affected from 0% (no movement) to 125% of normal servo travel. Normal servo travel is considered to be 45 degrees to each side of centre for a total servo range of 90 degrees. The factory default for each of the available EPAs is 100% of normal servo movement.

Now that you are in the EPA menu, select the channel to which you wish to make adjustments by pressing down on the right side of the Rudder (channel 4) trim switch until the channel number starts to flash on the display screen. Use the control stick to verify that the correct control surface is being affected. Since the Aileron channel (channel 1) is already flashing, we will start the EPA routine from there. Move the Aileron control stick to the right as far as it will go and hold it there; the LCD screen should now show 100%.

Using the Aileron (channel 1) trim switch, you may now increase this number to as much as 125% for maximum servo travel (press

the left side of the Aileron trim switch). Now move the aileron stick all the way to the left side, hold and repeat the process until you are satisfied with aileron movement.

Proceed to the next control surface by pressing the right side of the Rudder (channel 4) trim switch once to bring up the Elevator (channel 2) control surface, and repeat the process as you did for the Ailerons except that you will now be going up and down with the control stick instead of left and right.

Reminder: you will still use the Aileron trim switch to determine the percentage of servo travel.

Continue this process with each of the remaining control surfaces, then when you get to channel 5 please be advised that the End Point Adjustment will have no effect on a retract servo which is not proportional. It will have an effect on any other type of proportional servo and you can program EPAs to this channel.

Once you have finished all of the control surfaces to your

satisfaction, remember to scroll (using the UP or DN/TIMER key) to the SA (save) screen and press the CUT/SAVE key to save all the data. Two beeps will sound to confirm that it has been saved in the memory.

## LCD display

a. Press both UP and DN/TIMER keys down with main power switch ON.
b. Press either UP or DN/TIMER key until the display shows the End Point Adjustment menu.
c. Select desired channel by CH 4 trim.
d. Adjust End Point travel by CH 1 trim with selection direction of servo by control stick, knob or gear switch.
e. Go to the MAIN EDIT MODE SAVE menu by using either UP or DN/TIMER key and press CUT/SAVE key to save the input data.

Special note: When making the End Point Adjustments for the throttle servo, keep in mind that you will want to keep the carburettor slightly open at the extreme low end of the throttle control stick to ensure a reliable idle and to take best advantage of the Engine Cut feature, which will be discussed in more detail in the Trim Memory section.

Exponential rate adjustment, dual rate settings, servo reversing and trim memory reset are next described, and here are the instructions for Trim Memory, Aileron/ Rudder Mixing and Save Routine.

## Trim Memory

In this routine we can set all the control surfaces to a neutral setting prior to the first flight of the aircraft, then save all the trim input that was made during an actual flight. Because the Flash utilises digital trims as opposed to mechanical trims, you cannot see where the trims are set after a flight. You can, however, save all this data by simply accessing the MAIN EDIT MODE menu after a flight, scroll to the SA (save) screen and press CUT/SAVE to save all the trim settings. Therefore it is imperative that you do not turn off your transmitter after the initial trim-out flight until after you have saved the trim settings in the MAIN EDIT MODE menu.

To access this routine, use the UP key to scroll through to the TRM (trim memory) screen. The screen will display Channels 1 to 4 along the top with a percentage figure below that and TRM to the right of that figure. You can now set all your control surfaces to the neutral position prior to the initial flight of your aircraft.

As before, the Rudder trim switch will be used to select the channel and the Aileron trim switch will be used to set the control surface. If your displayed trim percentages end up near the 100% mark (+ or –) you may wish to adjust your mechanical linkages to obtain trim percentage figures closer to 0%. This will help maximise your total trim capability.

Scroll to the SA screen and save these settings. Once you get to the flying field, trim out the aircraft as you normally would, then land it and access the MAIN EDIT MODE menu. Scroll immediately to the SA screen and press the CUT/SAVE key to save your new trim settings. Your model should now be ready for its next flight.

LCD display:
a. Press both UP and DN/TIMER keys down with main power switch ON.
b. Press either UP or DN/TIMER key until the display shows the trim

memory menu.
c. Select desired channel by CH 4 trim.
d. Adjust neutral position by CH 1 trim.
e. Press CUT/SAVE key to memorise the neutral point of trim.
f. Go to the MAIN EDIT MODE SAVE menu by using either UP or DN/TIMER key and press CUT/SAVE key to save the i nput data.

Special note: To utilise the Engine Cut feature of this radio, start the motor (preferably at the flying field), then locate the idle point, as suggested by the engine manufacturer, using the Throttle trim with the Throttle stick all the way down. Once you have located this point, scroll to the SA screen and immediately save this setting prior to making your first flight. Now, with the engine still running at idle, press the CUT/SAVE key

and hold it down. The carburettor drum should be fully closed and the engine should shut down.

## Aileron/Rudder mixing

In the INITIAL MODE menu, you were given the option of three electronic mixing functions: Aileron/Rudder, Elevon and V-Tail. Of these three, only the Aileron/Rudder mix requires direct input from the modeller. Assuming that you have chosen this mix, let us proceed with this program.

Note: If you have not chosen to engage the Aileron/Rudder mix program from the INITIAL MODE menu, it will not appear on the menu screen sequence.

Aileron to Rudder mixing is commonly used to co-ordinate turns of large-scale aircraft and sailplanes. Within this program you may designate either of the two control channels as the 'master'

*On moving to the Aileron/Rudder mix menu, the OFF will be flashing. Press the channel 4 trim to change it to ON, then CUT/SAVE. Designate the 'slave' channel by pressing the channel 4 trim – Rudder is normally the 'slave' channel. By pressing the channel 1 trim the amount of rudder movement can be adjusted (holding the Aileron stick in the direction in which the adjustment is to be made). Check all of these mixing arrangements with the airborne equipment, ie the servo movements, then check carefully again when the gear is fitted in the model. It is possible to obtain reverse movements, ie left aileron – right rudder, designated by REV.*

with the other as the 'slave'. What this means is that if you designate the Aileron channel as the 'master', the Rudder channel will perform as the 'slave'. Whenever the Aileron stick is moved, the Rudder will move a preset amount in conjunction with the Ailerons in order to eliminate adverse yaw or to present a more scale-like turn for larger aircraft. However, it must be remembered that the Rudder ('slave') stick can over-ride any input from the Aileron ('master') stick at any time.

To begin programming of the Aileron/Rudder mix, use the UP key to scroll to AIL=RUD screen. The RUD message will be seen flashing in the lower left-hand corner with an OFF message directly above it. Press the Rudder (channel 4) trim switch on the left side once and the OFF message will start to flash. Now press the CUT/SAVE key and the message will read ON. Next press the Rudder trim switch to the right side once. The RUD message will now begin flashing with a value of 0% showing on the right side of the screen. If you intend to make the Rudder the 'slave' channel, you may proceed with the data input. If you wish to designate the Aileron channel as the 'slave', press the Rudder trim switch to the right one more time and the AIL message will now begin to flash.

Reminder: The channel that flashes on the LCD screen will be the 'slave' channel.

After designating the 'slave' channel, proceed as you did in setting up the EPAs. First, hold the 'master' control stick all the way to the left and use the Aileron (channel 1) trim switch to change the percentage being shown on the LCD screen. Notice that the screen will display the NOR (normal) or the REV (reverse) symbol to tell you which way the

'slaved' channel will move when the 'master' channel is operated. Normal rudder movement in this case means that when you give a left aileron command, you will also get a left rudder command. It is possible to get right rudder (or aileron) when left aileron (or rudder) is applied, so leave the receiver on and the servos plugged in to verify that the movement you desire is actually being input.

When you are satisfied that you have obtained the proper amount of left rudder input, proceed with the right rudder input. Hold the 'master' control stick all the way to the right and again use the Aileron trim switch to change the percentage being shown on the screen; check the servo movement to ensure that the 'slave' channel is moving in the proper direction. Once you have the proper mix percentage, scroll to the SA (save) screen and press CUT/SAVE to store the data.

LCD display:
a. Press both UP and DN/TIMER keys down with main power switch ON.

b. Press either UP or DN/TIMER key until the display shows the Aileron/Rudder mixing menu.
c. Press CH 4 trim on the left side once, and the OFF message will start to flash. Then press CUT/SAVE key to change the OFF to ON.
d. Designate the 'slave' channel by CH 4 trim. (The channel that flashes will be the 'slave'.)
e. Set the servo throw of the 'slave' channel aligned with the 'master' channel by CH 1 trim while indicating the servo direction with 'master' channel stick.
f. Go to the MAIN EDIT MODE SAVE menu by using either UP or DN/TIMER key and press CUT/SAVE key to save the input data.

Note: The other mixing options, V-Tail and Elevon, are considered linear mixes and the relationship between the channels remains constant. By eliminating the need for mechanical mixing devices, it is not necessary to program individual servo movement. Simply activate the mixing options from the INITIAL MODE menu and you're ready to go.

*After each programmed adjustment, when you are satisfied with it, the position is saved in the computer memory by moving to the SA (save) menu and pressing the CUT/SAVE key.*

## Save routine

The final routine available to you under the MAIN EDIT menu is the SA or save routine. Hopefully by this time you are quite familiar with this screen and that further explanation is unnecessary.

That last sentence says it all, and even if you have experienced a few problems in following all of the instructions from the printed page, I doubt whether you will have difficulties when you have the outfit by your side to watch cause and effect.

Once having grasped the principles of operation – and driven away the bogey of ignorance – it is a logical progression on to the more complex computerised systems.

*The voltage drops fairly rapidly from 9.6 volts to the danger voltage of 9.2 volts, when the bleeper sounds. If you are flying at that time, land immediately.*

# Appendix 4

# Frequency Allocations

Regrettably, the legal frequency allocations throughout the countries of the world do not show a commonality. Within certain areas there is a good degree of agreement on allocations, and in Europe, for instance, the 27MHz (for all models), 35MHz (aircraft), and 40MHz (surface vehicles) bands are in use in most countries. France is the main exception to this rule, which operates on 26MHz and two bands on the 41MHz frequencies.

The original allocations were nearly always on the 26/27MHz bands, but this became so contaminated with CB (Citizen Band) radio interference that, in many areas, it was unsafe to use this for model operation. As these wavebands are also used for the operation of traffic lights and other governmental and industrial purposes the use for modelling purposes can only be considered on a local basis.

The USA is also out on a limb as far as radio frequencies are concerned; they do not use 35 or 40MHz but have 72MHz – 72.030 to 72.430 for aircraft and 75MHz (75.430 to 75.710) for surface vehicles. They also permit operation on the 50 and 53MHz bands for holders of amateur radio licences. Australia and South Africa are also non-users of the 35MHz bands, their radio regulatory bodies allocating them bands in the 40 and 60MHz frequencies instead.

It seems doubtful that full international agreement over frequency allocation for R/C models will ever now be achieved. Modellers must accept the responsibility of ascertaining the legal frequency allocation and operating within those limits. Remember that all 'spot' frequencies within a band width may not be available for our purposes, and the omissions do not always have any logical pattern to them.

Each country will have a governing body for each modelling activity and these organisations should be able to confirm the legal frequencies in use. Often the governing body will be affiliated to an international body; for example, the British SMAE, American AMA, etc, will be affiliated to the FAI (Fédération Aeronautique International), and these organisations, too, should have the frequency information available.

Modellers travelling to other countries may have difficulty in obtaining frequency information from official sources. An alternative is to obtain a model magazine from the country in question and write to them for assistance.

# Appendix 5
# Dos and Don'ts

## Do . . .

1. Take time to investigate, understand, inspect and evaluate R/C outfits before purchasing.
2. Visit the local model club, ask what they use, ask whether it is satisfactory, ask what mode they use, ask whether they have a training scheme – and join.
3. Buy from a retailer from whom you can have a good back-up service; your first recourse if something is wrong with the equipment is to the retailer.
4. When you have purchased the equipment take plenty of time to read the instructions thoroughly, to understand them and to be able to translate them to the operation of the R/C equipment.
5. Plan your installation before commencing to construct the model. Be sure you know where all the components are to be fixed and the routes of the linkages.
6. Protect the receiver and battery by securing them firmly, but with a resilient protection. Arrange for alternative positions of these items if this is possible.
7. Fit servos where they can be easily accessed for changing or adjusting.
8. Keep all linkages as direct as possible and without excess free movement. Sloppy linkages will result in loss of accurate control.
9. Ensure that the linkages, control surfaces and wheels, etc, have no binding or limiting movement. Check for any problems and correct.
10. Make a neat and tidy installation – this will be best achieved by good pre-programming.
11. Keep the receiver as clear of wires and leads as possible and route the aerial away from other equipment.
12. Avoid metal-to-metal linkage connections, and keep radio equipment clear of spark ignition engines.
13. Follow the manufacturer's instructions regarding the radio equipment and the installation in the model – they have the experience.
14. Cycle the transmitter and receiver/servo batteries two or three times in the model before operating the model. Failures of equipment, linkages or hinges are more likely to show up in the first few hours.
15. Correct any faults found at this stage and replace any faulty items.
16. Check the range of the equipment on a regular basis.
17. Check the installation thoroughly after each modelling session.
18. Check again at the modelling site, after the model has been assembled.
19. Have your equipment inspected and serviced on a regular basis, preferably at the end of each season.
20. ENJOY YOURSELF – it's a hobby!

## Don't . . .

1. Be seduced into buying equipment unless it fully meets your requirements – ignore eager salesmen's patter.
2. Buy second-hand equipment unless it is demonstrated to you, or you can have a definite money-back guarantee if it is unsatisfactory.
3. Put brand new equipment into an expensive model; test it out in a 'hack' model first. Those first operations are where the faults – if any – will became apparent. The risk of faults is very small, but cannot be totally ignored.
4. Cram equipment into inaccessible areas where you can't ensure good protection.
5. Strain plug leads or aerial wires; use an extension lead where necessary.
6. Install an on/off switch where it can be contaminated by exhaust residues, oil or dirt.
7. Risk damage to equipment by water; protect the receiver, battery and servos with a suitable installation or plastic bags.
8. Over-tighten servo mounting or output arm screws.
9. Shorten receiver aerials – it will severely reduce the range, as will leaving the aerial in a coiled state.
10. Modify equipment – it will make the guarantee null and void.
11. Mix radio equipment of different makes, unless you know they are compatible.
12. Forget to fully charge the equipment, test then switch off until it is used.
13. Operate the equipment unless you have the appropriate frequency peg and it is safe.
14. Change crystals or frequency without remembering to change the frequency pennant on the transmitter.
15. Operate the model unless you are 100 per cent sure that everything is working 100 per cent.
16. Operate the model unless you have suitable insurance cover.
17. Operate the model without first making the necessary checks.
18. Operate on illegal frequencies, at unsuitable venues or when it entails risks to third parties.
19. Leave the model for long periods without disconnecting the battery. Store the equipment in a cold, damp atmosphere.
20. Operate the transmitter without fully extending the aerial – except for short periods when range checking.
21. Switch on the receiver until the transmitter has been switched on. The reverse is also true – the receiver should be switched off before the transmitter.

# Appendix 6
# Futaba PCM1024ZA/ZH Menu Glossary

Appendix 1 gives some of the more commonly used abbreviations for computor outfits but the top-of-the-range transmitters require a more extensive glossary. For example, this is the listing for the above outfit.

## Home Screen (HOM)

| | |
|---|---|
| S/S | Start/Stop timer |
| RST | Reset timer |
| TRM | Show trim menu |
| CHD | Condition hold |
| TIM | To timer menu |
| VLT | To voltmeter menu |
| TAC | To tach menu |
| T/R | Timer reset |
| SYS | To system menu |
| MDL | To model menu |
| CND | To condition menu |

## Other commands

| | |
|---|---|
| ACT | Activate |
| AUT | Auto |
| END | Return to previous menu |
| INH | Inhibit |
| LIN | Linear |
| LST | Last part of list |
| MAN | Manual |
| NXT | Next menu |
| PRE | Previous menu |
| PT → | Next point to right |
| ← PT | Next point to left |
| RST | Reset menu |
| SEL | Select |
| SET | Yes, command is OK |
| SRV | Servo |

| | |
|---|---|
| SWT | To switch set menu |
| VOL | To volume set menu |
| [+/-] | Change sign |
| [+] | Add 1 |
| [-] | Subtract 1 |
| [nnn] | Inputs number 'nnn' |

## Transmitter abbreviations

| | |
|---|---|
| J1 | Right stick horizontal |
| J2 | Right stick vertical |
| J3 | Left stick vertical |
| J4 | Left stick horizontal |
| RS | Right slider |
| LS | Left slider |
| RD | Right dial VR(A) |
| LD | Left dial (B) |
| SW(n) | Switch No. (n) |

## System menu [SYS]

| | |
|---|---|
| MSL | Model selection |
| VLT | Voltmeter |
| OFF | No load |
| 250 | 250 mA load |
| 500 | 500 mA load |
| TAC | Tachometer |
| DSP | Display on/off |
| SRV | Servo Test and Bar graph display |
| ON | Activation function |
| OFF | Switch off |
| TRN | Trainer system/command |
| MIX | Mix trainer commands |
| DTN | Data transfer |
| TRN | Transmit model data |

| | |
|---|---|
| RCV | Receive model data |
| CPM | Copy model |
| CPC | Copy condition |
| PAR | Parameters |
| UNA | User name def. |
| ENT | Enter letter at cursor |
| FRQ | Transmitter frequency setting (Syn. only) |
| ABT | Abort setting |

## Model menu [MDL]

| | |
|---|---|
| CSL | Condition select |
| TIM | Timer function |
| UP | Set timer count up |
| DWN | Set timer countdown |
| S/S | Start/Stop timer |
| RST | Reset timer |
| F/S | Failsafe function |
| BFS | Battery failsafe |
| NOR | Hold last command |
| PMD | Pulse mode |
| PCM | Pulse code modulation |
| PPM | Pulse position modulation (FM) |
| REV | Servo reversing Rev. selected servo |
| FNC | Function change |
| TRM | Trim tab |
| CTR | Control stick/knob |
| RST | Data reset |
| CUT | Engine cut |
| CHD | Condition hold |
| TYP | Model type selection |
| CH9 | Channel 9 switch |
| MNA | Model name def. |

| | |
|---|---|
| ALT | Alternate switch |
| THR | Throttle curve |
| SWH | Swashplate type |
| S-1 | Normal swash |
| S-2, 4 | Mixed swash type 2, 4 |
| SN3 | Swash type SN3 |
| SR3 | Swash type SR3 |
| RDR | Rotor direction |
| CW | Clockwise |
| CCW | Counterclockwise |
| INV | Inverted pitch |
| PIT | Pitch curve |

## Common conditions [CND]

| | |
|---|---|
| CSL | Condition select |
| ATV | Adjustable travel volume, Channel delay |
| NOR | Normal |
| LIM | Limited |
| AFR | Adjustable function rate |
| D/R | Dual rate |
| PMX | Programmable mixing |
| STM | Sub trim |
| TOF | Trim offset |
| CNA | Condition naming |
| TRM | Digital trim |
| T1-4 | Trims 1 – 4 |
| C-M | Current to memory |
| M-C | Memory into current |
| ATL | Trim at low end only |
| CMB | Combined all conds. |
| SEP | Trim this cond. only |

## Model type labels

| | |
|---|---|
| AIR | Aeroplane type |
| HEL | Helicopter type |
| GL2 | Sailplane, 2 wing servos |
| GL4 | Sailplane, 4 wing servos |
| GL5 | Sailplane, 5 wing servos |

## Aeroplane menu

| | |
|---|---|
| ADF | Aileron differential |
| A → R | Aileron → Rudder mixing |
| VTL | V-tail mixing |
| R → A | Rudder → Aileron mixing |
| EVN | Elevon |
| E → F | Elevator → Flap mixing |
| F → E | Flap → Elevator mixing |
| CPT | Collective pitch |
| ALV | Ailevator |
| FPN | Flaperon |
| ABK | Air brake |
| SPO | Spoiler control |
| AUT | Automatic mode |
| MAN | Manual mode |
| SNP | Snap roll |
| TCV | Throttle curve |

## Sailplane menu

| | |
|---|---|
| ADF | Aileron differential |
| A → R | Rudder coupling |
| ASF | Aileron → Speed flap mixing |
| VTL | V-tail mixing |
| ABE | Airbrake |
| EBF | Elevator → Brake flap mixing |
| ESF | Elevator → Speed flap mixing |
| BKF | Brake flap |
| SPF | Speed flap |
| SFT | Flap trim setting |
| BFY | Butterfly |
| BYE | Butterfly trim mixing |
| ETM | Elevator trim sets |
| TM1 | Trim set 1 |
| TM2 | Trim set 2 |
| F → E | Flap → Elevator mixing |
| E → F | Elevator → Flap mixing |
| FPN | Flaperon mixing |

## Helicopter menu

| | |
|---|---|
| PCV | Pitch mixing |
| PHV | Hovering pitch |
| PTM | Pitch trim |
| TCV | Throttle curve |
| THV | Hovering throttle |
| HOF | Hovering offset |
| HLD | Throttle hold |
| SWP | Swashplate type |
| P → R | Pitch → Rudder |
| R → T | Rudder → Throttle |
| GYR | Gyro sensitivity |
| ACC | Acceleration |
| INV | Inverted pitch |

## Model control abbreviations

| | |
|---|---|
| AIL | Aileron |
| AU1 | Aux Channel 1 |
| AU2 | Aux Channel 2 |
| BKF | Brake flap |
| CH9 | Channel 9 |
| ELE | Elevator |
| FLP | Flap |
| GEA | Gear |
| GYR | Gyro |
| PIT | Pitch |
| RUD | Rudder |
| SF1 | Speed flap 1 |
| SF2 | Speed flap 2 |
| SPO | Spoiler |
| THR | Throttle |

## Miscellaneous abbreviations

| | |
|---|---|
| Syn | Synthesized |

*Note: Indented entries are subcommands*

# Appendix 7

# Useful addresses

Civil Aviation Authority (CAA)
General Aviation Section,
Aviation House, South Area,
Gatwick Airport, Gatwick,
West Sussex RH6 0YR

British Model Flying Association
(BMFA)
Chacksfield House,
31 St Andrews Road,
Leicester LE2 8RE

British Association of Radio
Control Soarers (BARCS)
c/o 51 Crutchfield Lane,
Walton-on-Thames,
Surrey KT12 2QY

British Electric Flight Association
c/o 1 Linwood Avenue,
Tolsburg, Middlesbrough,
Cleveland TS5 7RD

British Miniature Pylon Racing
Association (BMPRA)
c/o 6 Ullerwater Drive,
Spring Meadows, Gamston,
Nottingham.

British Waterplane Association
(BWA)
c/o The Hollies,
48 New Street, Kenilworth,
Warwickshire CV8 2EZ

Club Twenty Association (CTA)
c/o 9 Shelley Gardens, Hinckley,
Leics LE10 1TA

Great Britain Radio Control
Aerobatic Association (GBRCA)
c/o 84 Hollymoor Road,
Hollymoorside, Chesterfield,
S42 7DX

British Radio Control Helicopter
Association (BRCHA)
c/o 7 Kiln Way, Badger Drive,
Grays, Essex RM17 5JE

Society of Antique Modellers
(SAM35)
c/o 9 Queens Road, Wellington,
Somerset TA21 9AW

Scottish Association of
Aeromodellers
c/o 2 Forth Avenue, Kirkaldy,
Scotland KY2 5PN

Northern Ireland Association
of Aeromodellers
c/o 28 Colston Avenue, Holywood,
Co. Down, N. Ireland

Model Pilots Association (MPA)
Nexus House, Boundary Way,
Hemel Hempstead,
Herts HP2 7ST

**Magazine and book publishers**

Nexus Specialist Interests
Nexus House, Boundary Way,
Hemel Hempstead,
Herts HP2 7ST

Model Activity Press Ltd
33 Start Street, Ware,
Herts SG12 7AA

Traplet Publications Ltd
Traplet House, Severn Drive,
Upton-on-Severn,
Worcs WR8 0JL

# Acknowledgements

I would like to acknowledge the
assistance of the following persons
and companies in providing
information, illustrations and
encouragement in compiling
this book.

Futaba Corporation, Japan

JR Propo, Japan

Kyosko, Japan

Robbe, Germany

Avevang Ltd, Commerce Way,
Lancing, West Sussex BN15 8TE

Chart Hobby Distributors Ltd,
Chart House, Station Road,
East Preston, Littlehampton,
West Sussex BN16 3AG

Flair Products, Holdcroft Works,
Blunsdon, Swindon,
Wiltshire SN2 4AH

Fleet Control Systems
47 Fleet Road, Fleet,
Hampshire GU13 8PJ

Irvine Engines Ltd, Unit 2,
Brunswick Industrial Park,
Brunswick Way, New Southgate,
London N11 1JL

MacGregor Industries Ltd,
Canal Estate, Langley,
Berks SL3 6EQ

Mainlink Systems
1 Blunham Road, Moggerhanger,
Bedford MK44 3RD

Nexus Specialist Interests
Nexus House, Boundary Way,
Hemel Hemspstead,
Herts HP2 7ST

Ripmax Models PLC
Ripmax Corner, Green Street,
Enfield, London EN3 7SJ

John Cundell

Alan Harman